MW01248099

Meet My God

He Is My Lord,
My Heavenly Father,
and My BFF

by

Lystra M. Williams

Trilogy Christian Publishers

A Wholly Owned Subsidary of Trinity Broadcasting Network

2442 Michelle Drive

Tustin, CA 92780

Copyright © 2019 by Lystra M. Williams

All Scripture quotations, unless otherwise noted, taken from THE HOLY BIBLE, NEW INTERNATIONAL VERSION®, NIV® Copyright © 1973, 1978, 1984, 2011 by Biblica, Inc.® Used by permission. All rights reserved worldwide.

Scripture quotations marked (KJV) taken from The Holy Bible, King James Version. Cambridge Edition: 1769.

All rights reserved, including the right to reproduce this book or portions thereof in any form whatsoever.

For information, address Trilogy Christian Publishing

Rights Department, 2442 Michelle Drive, Tustin, Ca 92780.

Trilogy Christian Publishing/ TBN and colophon are trademarks of Trinity Broadcasting Network.

For information about special discounts for bulk purchases, please contact Trilogy Christian Publishing.

Manufactured in the United States of America

Trilogy Disclaimer: The views and content expressed in this book are those of the author and may not necessarily reflect the views and doctrine of Trilogy Christian Publishing or the Trinity Broadcasting Network.

10 9 8 7 6 5 4 3 2 1

Library of Congress Cataloging-in-Publication Data is available.

B-ISBN#: 978-1-64088-215-7

E-ISBN#: 978-1-64088-216-4

Who is like you, Lord God Almighty?
You, Lord, are mighty, and your faithfulness surrounds you.
You rule over the surging sea; when its
waves mount up, you still them.
The heavens are yours, and yours also the earth; you
founded the world and all that is in it.
Psalm 89:8, 9, 11

Table of Contents

1
His Name Is

"I am the Lord. I appeared to Abraham, to Isaac and to Jacob as God Almighty, but by my name the Lord I did not make myself fully known to them."

Exodus 6:2-3

I would like to introduce you to my God...the Lord...my Heavenly Father...my best friend forever. He has told us that his name is "The Lord," according to the English translation of the Bible. In the original language, his name was and is a four-letter word (YHWH), which means past, present, and future; but the true essence indicates that he transcends time and exists in the past, present, and future simultaneously. If we can wrap our finite minds around this fact, then we can understand why the Jews would not say his real name. Out of respect, reverence, and honor for him, they chose to refer to him by descriptive names, such as Israel's King and Redeemer, the Holy One of Israel, the God of all the earth, the true God, the living God, the eternal King, the Alpha and the Omega, and more.

Bible scholars will tell you that there are sixteen names of God used throughout the Bible:

- Elohim (God)
- Yahweh (Lord, Jehovah)
- El Elyon (The Most High God)
- Adonai (Lord, Master)
- El Shaddai (Lord God Almighty)
- El Olam (Everlasting God)
- Jehovah Jireh (The Lord Will Provide)
- Jehovah Rapha (The Lord Who Heals You)

- Jehovah Nissi (The Lord Is My Banner)
- El Qanna (Jealous God)
- Jehovah Mekoddishkem (The Lord Who Sanctifies)
- Jehovah Shalom (The Lord Is Peace)
- Jehovah Sabaoth (The Lord of Hosts)
- Jehovah Raah (The Lord Is My Shepherd)
- Jehovah Tsidkenu (The Lord Our Righteousness)
- Jehovah Shammah (The Lord Is There)

These are all descriptive names of God used throughout the Bible. However, I have noticed that each prophet in the Bible had a preferred name for our God. For instance, Jeremiah referred to him quite often as "The Lord God Almighty, the God of Israel," while Ezekiel referred to him as "The Sovereign Lord" and Daniel referred to him as "The Ancient of Days."

I call him Father or Lord, but to me he is so much more than any one name. In the same way that he is past, present, and future all at once, he knows everything, is everywhere, can do anything, and has already thought of everything for me ahead of time. Once we get past the need to give him a name or to know his real name, we can really get into knowing him, or at least experiencing him. After all, what is in a name? It is supposed to identify a person or a thing from other things that are similar to it, but God is one of a kind. There is no other God, so does he really need a name? There is only one true God. There are imitations or false representations, but only one real God. He has told us that over and over.

> *"This is what the Lord says—*
> *Israel's King and Redeemer, the Lord Almighty:*
> *I am the first and I am the last;*
> *apart from me there is no God."*

Isaiah 44:6

> *For this is what the Lord says—*
> *he who created the heavens,*
> * he is God;*
> *he who fashioned and made the earth,*
> * he founded it*
> *he did not create it to be empty,*
> * but formed it to be inhabited—*

he says:
"I am the Lord,
*   and there is no other."*

Isaiah 45:18

Acknowledge and take to heart this day that the Lord is God in heaven
above and on the earth below. There is no other.

Deuteronomy 4:39

King David liked to refer to God as "the Lord of hosts" or "the Lord of Heaven's Armies," and many other prophets, including Isaiah, Jeremiah, and Amos, also used this name for the Lord. When David came to fight Goliath the giant, he wanted to convey to Goliath that the God of Israel's army was no wimp. He is much more than the God of Israel; he is God of the hosts of heaven and God of heaven's armies, so Goliath needed to realize who it was that he was defying.

David replied to the Philistine, "You come to me with sword, spear,
and javelin, but I come to you in the name of the LORD of Heaven's
Armies—the God of the armies of Israel, whom you have defied.

1 Samuel 17:45(NLT)

That was a powerful statement. Israel may only have one earthly army, but God has numerous heavenly armies to fight on behalf of Israel. He is the *God of the armies of Israel.*

My God and Father is definitely not a figment of the imagination. He has appeared to many men in the Bible, and we have clear descriptions from them about these encounters. The stories of the Bible are embedded in verifiable historical events but are told from the perspective of an all-knowing God. Why did God go through so much trouble to show himself to the people of Israel? He told Moses why.

The Lord said to Moses, "I am going to come to you in a dense cloud,
so that the people will hear me speaking with you and will always put
their trust in you."

Exodus 19:9

God knew that some would say that the Bible was written by men who wanted to control people with religion. So, he appeared to several men so that we would have some evidence to believe. We read in Genesis that the Lord used to come down on evenings and walk with Adam in the Garden of Eden (Genesis 3:8). It is obvious that he is seeking a relationship with us. Such a big God could just send an angel to fetch us to Himself; but no, He chose to come down to our level to foster a relationship with us. He also visited with Abraham on his way to destroy Sodom and Gomorrah. We are told that he chose to share his thoughts and intentions regarding Sodom and Gomorrah with Abraham. (Genesis 18). Jacob, Abraham's grandson, also had several personal encounters with the Lord. At least three times he encountered God in what Jacob called the Gateway to Heaven (Genesis 28:12-17, Genesis 32:24-30 and Genesis 35:9-10 NLT).

However, when God decided to show himself to his people, he was not disguised in the form of a man, but he came in his full power and glory. The Lord told Moses he had chosen the descendants of Abraham to be his special treasure (Exodus 19:3-6), and he wanted them to have their own encounter with their God so that it would be more than hearsay. So, he passed by and spoke to them from Mount Sinai. That first mass revelation did not go too well. The people were scared and asked that God speak only to Moses in the future. Then Moses would speak to them.

They took this opportunity for granted. It was a very big deal. God later spoke about it as being one of the greatest things to have ever happened up to that point.

Ask now about the former days, long before your time, from the day God created human beings on the earth; ask from one end of the heavens to the other. Has anything so great as this ever happened, or has anything like it ever been heard of? Has any other people heard the voice of God speaking out of fire, as you have, and lived?

Deuteronomy 4:32-33

Despite that rebuff, the Lord still had Moses bring about seventy elders up on the mountain for a closer encounter with him.

Moses and Aaron, Nadab and Abihu, and the seventy elders of Israel went up and saw the God of Israel. Under his feet was something like a pavement made of lapis lazuli, as bright blue as the sky. But God did not raise his hand against these leaders of the Israelites; they saw God, and they ate and drank.

The Lord said to Moses, "Come up to me on the mountain and stay here, and I will give you the tablets of stone with the law and commandments I have written for their instruction."

Then Moses set out with Joshua his aide, and Moses went up on the mountain of God. He said to the elders, "Wait here for us until we come back to you. Aaron and Hur are with you, and anyone involved in a dispute can go to them."

When Moses went up on the mountain, the cloud covered it, and the glory of the Lord settled on Mount Sinai. For six days the cloud covered the mountain, and on the seventh day the Lord called to Moses from within the cloud. To the Israelites the glory of the Lord looked like a consuming fire on top of the mountain. Then Moses entered the cloud as he went on up the mountain. And he stayed on the mountain forty days and forty nights.

Exodus 24:9-18

The prophet Ezekiel also had several encounters with the "One who sits on a Throne." (Ezekiel 1, Ezekiel 3:22-25, Ezekiel 8-11). He wrote the most graphic description of the beings he encountered. In the first chapter of Ezekiel, he described his encounter by the Kebar River in Babylon. The chariot-like vehicle with wheels came from the sky in what seemed like a huge windstorm. He told about the four beings with wings that controlled the wheels. Each of these beings had four different faces. Above the wheels was a shiny vault, and above the vault was the lapis lazuli throne, where the Lord or the glory of God sat. He wrote,

Then there came a voice from above the vault over their heads as they stood with lowered wings. Above the vault over their heads was what looked like a throne of lapis lazuli, and high above on the throne was a figure like that of a man. I saw that from what appeared to be his waist up he looked like glowing metal, as if full of fire, and that from there down he looked like fire; and brilliant light surrounded him. Like the appearance of a rainbow in the clouds on a rainy day, so was the radiance around him. This was the appearance of the likeness of the glory of the Lord. When I saw it, I fell facedown, and I heard the voice of one speaking.

Ezekiel 1:25-28

They all described the Lord as having a blue lapis lazuli stone under his feet or in his throne. Is it any wonder that the skies are blue? Scientists say that space is black. The blue skies and our blue earth are signs that God is with us.

In Daniel 10-12, Daniel only spoke with an angel, but the experience was so much more than our human bodies were meant to tolerate. It left him weak and trembling with fear, and he had to be touched to restore his strength.

On April 23, as I was standing on the bank of the great Tigris River, I looked up and saw a man dressed in linen clothing, with a belt of pure gold around his waist. His body looked like a precious gem. His face flashed like lightning, and his eyes flamed like torches. His arms and feet shone like polished bronze, and his voice roared like a vast multitude of people.

Only I, Daniel, saw this vision. The men with me saw nothing, but they were suddenly terrified and ran away to hide. So, I was left there all alone to see this amazing vision. My strength left me, my face grew deathly pale, and I felt very weak. Then I heard the man speak, and when I heard the sound of his voice, I fainted and lay there with my face to the ground.

Just then a hand touched me and lifted me, still trembling, to my hands and knees. And the man said to me, "Daniel, you are very precious to God, so listen carefully to what I have to say to you. Stand up, for I have been sent to you." When he said this to me, I stood up, still trembling.

Then he said, "Don't be afraid, Daniel. Since the first day you began to pray for understanding and to humble yourself before your God, your request has been heard in heaven. I have come in answer to your prayer. But for twenty-one days the spirit prince of the kingdom of Persia blocked my way. Then Michael, one of the archangels, came to help me, and I left him there with the spirit prince of the kingdom of Persia. Now I am here to explain what will happen to your people in the future, for this vision concerns a time yet to come."

While he was speaking to me, I looked down at the ground, unable to say a word. Then the one who looked like a man touched my lips, and I opened my mouth and began to speak. I said to the one standing in front of me, "I am filled with anguish because of the vision I have seen, my lord, and I am very weak. How can someone like me, your servant, talk to you, my lord? My strength is gone, and I can hardly breathe." Then the one who looked like a man touched me again, and I felt my strength returning. "Don't be afraid," he said, "for you are very precious to God. Peace! Be encouraged! Be strong!"

As he spoke these words to me, I suddenly felt stronger and said to him, "Please speak to me, my lord, for you have strengthened me."
Daniel 10:4-19 NLT

What we can gather from all of this is that these spiritual beings can manifest themselves in whatsoever form they choose. Sometimes, they come in all their heavenly glory; but at other times, they would appear as men.

My encounter with an angel was far less dramatic, but very effective. One day, when I had just moved to Brooklyn, New York, I had spent the last of my money on a train ride to get home. The train came to a stop at a station, and everyone was told that they had to get off at that station. I knew that if I left that platform, I would not have the money to transfer to another train, so I hung around, fearful and not knowing what to do.

My eyes filled with tears, and just as everyone else had left the platform, a man in strange clothes from another era came up to me and asked if I was all right. I told him what the problem was, and he directed me to stay on the platform, that another train would soon come by to take me home. I thanked him and looked away for a second. When I looked back, he had vanished and I was alone again on the platform.

As I shivered from the cold I was not accustomed to, I thought about how strange his garments were. He had no overcoat, and his white, long-sleeve shirt still had creases in it. He was not a local traveler. He was an angel sent to guide me and calm my fears in my time of need.

Paul warned us to be nice to others, because many have entertained angels and were unaware of it.

Don't forget to show hospitality to strangers, for some who have done this have entertained angels without realizing it!'

Hebrews 13:2 NLT

The Lord knew that people would find it hard to believe without seeing, or at least hearing the voice of the God they serve. We have the "Doubting Thomas" mentality. When the disciples told Thomas they had seen the risen Jesus, he replied, *"I won't believe it unless I see the nail wounds in his hands, put my fingers into them, and place my hand into the wound in his side"* (John 20:25 NLT).

When Jesus later appeared to Thomas and he believed, Jesus told him, *"You believe because you have seen me. Blessed are those who believe without seeing me"* (John 20:29 NLT).

A former Hindu co-worker had, in the middle of her desk, a small, white ornament with the image of a pearl white horse embossed on it. When I asked her about it, she said proudly that it was her god. All day long, I could hear her whispering, "My god." She needed to see her god constantly, and we can fall into the same trap of needing to see the Living God. When the children of Israel made the golden calf and said that this calf had brought them out of Egypt, they were trying to create a visible God and give it the attributes of the real God. They had just had an encounter with the real God of the Universe and heard his voice. Moses had told them the things God had told him. He even wrote it down for them.

> *When Moses went and told the people all the Lord's words and laws, they responded with one voice, "Everything the Lord has said we will do." Moses then wrote down everything the Lord had said.*
>
> *Exodus 24:3-4*

Although the instructions Moses gave them included the Ten Commandments — where God had said that they were not to have any other gods before Him, make images of anything in heaven or earth, or bow down to any images — when they had to wait for Moses for a few days, they tried to keep their experience fresh by applying what they had seen the Egyptians do for their gods. They made an image of their god and worshiped the image the way they knew how.

The Lord...the real God...told them not to do this.

> *After they have been destroyed before you, be careful not to be ensnared by inquiring about their gods, saying, "How do these nations serve*

their gods? We will do the same." You must not worship the Lord your God in their way, because in worshiping their gods, they do all kinds of detestable things the Lord hates. They even burn their sons and daughters in the fire as sacrifices to their gods. See that you do all I command you; do not add to it or take away from it.

Deuteronomy 12:30-32

No image could ever emulate the fullness of the Godhead. The Lord is omniscient (he knows everything), eternal (he has no beginning or end), and omnipresent (he is everywhere at the same time). If you have an image, you may forget that the Lord is not limited like the image. The image does not know anything, the image can be broken and is not eternal, and the image can only be in one place at a time.

Some may not create a physical image, but they worship a mental image of God. They are taught that God is a loving God who conforms to our imagination of how he should behave. When a disaster happens, they ask, "How could a loving God allow such pain and suffering?" They forget that this loving God is also an all-powerful God, who destroyed all the sinful people of Noah's day except for Noah and his family. They have not heard that this same God opened the earth and swallowed up a group of Levites and all their belongings when they challenged Moses about the priesthood. The Lord is not our equal, and we should not expect him to act like us. We should respect and fear him and not challenge him.

Do not make any images of God, mental or otherwise, or we reduce him to the level of these fake gods that others worship. Accept the fact that he is invisible and eternal and stop trying to bring him down to our level.

This God being, my Lord and my God, who is so unlike us and so far beyond us, still pursues us, even though he knows our shortcomings. He made us, so he already knows everything there is to know about us; yet he is willing to invest his love in such ungrateful and unloving beings. It is no wonder John said, "Whoever does not love does not know God, because God is love" (1 John 4:8).

The amazing thing is that the more we truly know him, the more we love him and love others as well. It is as though we cannot help ourselves. We become more like him, and we love what he loves and want to help others.

It is this miraculous change in us that is the greatest evidence of God's existence. The act of believing in a God that we have only heard about but have not seen is rewarded beyond our imagination. Jesus said that we would be blessed when we believed without seeing, but that is only the beginning. It is a whole new existence. That is what is referred to as "the new birth." This belief is called faith, and "Without faith it is impossible to please God, because anyone who comes to him must believe that he exists and that he rewards those who earnestly seek him" (Hebrews 11:6).

That is why I am excited for you to meet my God, the Lord. You may not be able to see him physically right now, but you must come to him with the mind of a child. This amazing experience begins with just believing. This is what Jesus meant when he said, "Truly I tell you, unless you change and become like little children, you will never enter the kingdom of heaven" (Matthew 18:3).

A world of wondrous experiences and encounters await you beyond that point. Millions have already experienced it and are being changed as they encounter this God, the Lord, my Heavenly Father and my best friend forever.

2
He is a Great and Awesome God

For the Lord your God is God of gods and Lord of lords, the great God, mighty and awesome, who shows no partiality and accepts no bribes.
Deuteronomy 10:17

Jesus once accused the Samaritans of worshiping what they did not know.

"You Samaritans worship what you do not know; we worship what we do know, for salvation is from the Jews."
John 4:22

Yet, so many of us today still worship what we do not know. We do not even question why we worship whom or what, except that we have been told that we ought to worship. We have been created with a need to worship, so we find something...anything...to worship.

We should, however, know the God that we worship. It is like fitting the right peg in the right hole. You will not be satisfied until you find the right God to worship. We should ask questions about why we worship whom we worship. With that in mind, I would like to tell you why my God, the Lord, is worthy of worship.

When my Hindu co-worker worships her little white ornament, the only attribute she can honestly say that her god has is that it is pleasing to the eye. Beyond that, it can do nothing. If it is to be moved, she has to move it. If it is to be cleaned, she has to clean it. It is only wishful thinking to believe that something that is made by man can actually affect her life for good or evil.

On the other hand, the psalmist, Ethan, wrote about my God, the Lord,

The heavens praise your wonders, Lord,
   your faithfulness too, in the assembly of the holy ones.
For who in the skies above can compare with the Lord?
   Who is like the Lord among the heavenly beings?
In the council of the holy ones God is greatly feared;
   he is more awesome than all who surround him.
Who is like you, Lord God Almighty?
   You, Lord, are mighty, and your faithfulness surrounds you.
You rule over the surging sea;
   when its waves mount up, you still them.
You crushed Rahab like one of the slain;
   with your strong arm you scattered your enemies.
The heavens are yours, and yours also the earth;
   you founded the world and all that is in it.
You created the north and the south.

Psalm 89:5-12

My God, the Lord, created the heavens and the earth. He created the animals and humans. He controls the sea, the sun, and all the elements. He turned back time for Hezekiah (2 Kings 20:8-11), created a storm to re-route Jonah (Jonah 1:3-6), made a ten-mile path in the Red Sea, so that his people could cross over on dry ground (Exodus 14), and calmed the storm when Jesus said, "Peace, be still," to the storm. (Mark 4:35-39). Yes, my God, the Lord, has demonstrated that he has full control over the elements of this world. He did not just say it, or wish it, he does it all.

If I am going to entrust my life and my well-being to someone, I would choose the Lord, because he has proven that he has full control. Even in this era that is post-Bible, he continues to demonstrate his power and ability by raising people from the dead, growing limbs, and opening blind eyes — all in response to our prayers. There is evidence all around us that he is a super God. We worship some men for far less than this.

It does not matter how many great things the Lord, my God, has done; we still want to know what he can do for us. There are many great stories recorded in the Bible that tell us what our God is capable of doing. If he can do it for others, he can definitely do it for us. We just need to trust him.

He is worthy of our worship just for these amazing and awe-inspiring acts, and when such a mighty God also shows a loving and tender side, it makes him even more worthy of our adoration. He is beckoning us to come to him and be safe and blessed. He even promises rewards for those who genuinely seek him. The apostle Paul said, *"He that comes to God must believe that he is, and that he is a rewarder of those who diligently seek him"* (Hebrews 11:6 NKJV)

When God made the covenant with the Jews in the wilderness, he did not only give them a lot of laws to keep, but he gave them an incentive to keep the laws. He could have just said, "I am God, and you have to do as I say, or else I will destroy you." Instead, he lovingly promised them that if they would love him, walk in his ways, and seek him, he would greatly reward them.

> *"So if you faithfully obey the commands I am giving you today—to love the Lord your God and to serve him with all your heart and with all your soul—then I will send rain on your land in its season, both autumn and spring rains, so that you may gather in your grain, new wine and olive oil. I will provide grass in the fields for your cattle, and you will eat and be satisfied.*

> *If you carefully observe all these commands I am giving you to follow— to love the Lord your God, to walk in obedience to him and to hold fast to him—then the Lord will drive out all these nations before you, and you will dispossess nations larger and stronger than you. Every place where you set your foot will be yours: Your territory will extend from the desert to Lebanon, and from the Euphrates River to the Mediterranean Sea. No one will be able to stand against you. The Lord your God, as He promised you, will put the terror and fear of you on the whole land, wherever you go.*

> *See, I am setting before you today a blessing and a curse—the blessing if you obey the commands of the Lord your God that I am giving you today; the curse if you disobey the commands of the Lord your God.*
> *Deuteronomy 11:13-15, 22-28*

God kept his promises too. When they kept their end of the agreement, he rewarded them exactly as he had promised; however, when they turned to serving other gods, they came under a curse. The Jews are a people who have been blessed and continue to be blessed more than any other people.

It is no wonder they are so hated by some nations. They have the favor of God in their lives, and they prosper in whatever they do. By the same stretch, they are also a people that has experienced more pain and suffering than most other nations: slavery, holocaust, and anti-Semitism. They have experienced the extremes needlessly. You see...

> *The Lord is not slow in keeping his promise, as some understand slowness. Instead he is patient with you, not wanting anyone to perish, but everyone to come to repentance.*
>
> *2 Peter 3:9*

The Lord is waiting for them to return to him so he can bless them. He does not want to see them cursed, but he is bound by his word. He is a holy God, which has its benefits. We can trust whatever he says, be it good or bad. We just need to learn to be more like him and keep the promises we make to him.

My God, the Lord, wants to bless us. He often used the analogy of a shepherd and his sheep to describe our relationship with him. King David wrote,

> *The Lord is my shepherd, I lack nothing.*
> *   He makes me lie down in green pastures,*
> *he leads me beside quiet waters,*
> *   he refreshes my soul.*
> *He guides me along the right paths*
> *   for his name's sake.*
> *Even though I walk*
> *   through the darkest valley,*
> *I will fear no evil,*
> *   for you are with me*
> *your rod and your staff,*
> *   they comfort me.*
> *You prepare a table before me*
> *   in the presence of my enemies.*
> *You anoint my head with oil;*
> *   my cup overflows.*
> *Surely your goodness and love will follow me*
> *   all the days of my life,*

and I will dwell in the house of the Lord
  forever."

Psalm 23

David enjoyed being a kept and protected man. Like a shepherd that watched over his sheep and protected them from every danger, David envisioned himself living the good life with no worry, because his God, the Lord, would take care of his every need.

Jesus also told us that we can live without worry.

"Do not worry about your life, what you will eat or drink; or about your body, what you will wear. Is not life more than food, and the body more than clothes? Look at the birds of the air; they do not sow or reap or store away in barns, and yet your heavenly Father feeds them. Are you not much more valuable than they? Can any one of you by worrying add a single hour to your life?

And why do you worry about clothes? See how the flowers of the field grow. They do not labor or spin. Yet I tell you that not even Solomon in all his splendor was dressed like one of these. If that is how God clothes the grass of the field, which is here today and tomorrow is thrown into the fire, will he not much more clothe you—you of little faith? So do not worry, saying, 'What shall we eat?' or 'What shall we drink?' or 'What shall we wear?' For the pagans run after all these things, and your heavenly Father knows that you need them. But seek first His kingdom and His righteousness, and all these things will be given to you as well. Therefore, do not worry about tomorrow, for tomorrow will worry about itself. Each day has enough trouble of its own."
Matthew 6:25-34

If we understand this, life becomes easy and stress-free. We do not have to worry about anything but serving our God and our Lord. He will take care of everything else. To get to that point and that relationship, we must first believe that God is, and that he is the rewarder of those who diligently seek him (Hebrews 11:6).

Moses met with God on a regular basis during the forty-year trip to the Promised Land. When he said, "The Lord your God is God of gods and Lord of lords, the great God, mighty and awesome, who shows no partiality and accepts no bribes" (Deuteronomy 10:17), we ought to believe him. He even qualified these statements by explaining why he thought so.

He defends the cause of the fatherless and the widow, and loves the foreigner residing among you, giving them food and clothing.
Deuteronomy 10:18

Moreover, the Lord your God will send the hornet among them until even the survivors who hide from you have perished. Do not be terrified by them, for the Lord your God, who is among you, is a great and awesome God. The Lord your God will drive out those nations before you, little by little. You will not be allowed to eliminate them all at once, or the wild animals will multiply around you.
Deuteronomy 7:20-22

Isaiah confirmed that the Lord is a great and awesome God, and no one else can compare to him in heaven or on earth.

Do you not know?
  Have you not heard?
The Lord is the everlasting God,
  the Creator of the ends of the earth.
He will not grow tired or weary,
  and his understanding no one can fathom.
Isaiah 40:28

David also was amazed at God's ability to be everywhere and to know everything about us. He said,

You have searched me, Lord,
  and you know me.
You know when I sit and when I rise;
  you perceive my thoughts from afar.
You discern my going out and my lying down;
  you are familiar with all my ways.
Before a word is on my tongue,
  you, Lord, know it completely.
You hem me in behind and before,
  and you lay your hand upon me.

Such knowledge is too wonderful for me,
  too lofty for me to attain.

Where can I go from your Spirit?
  Where can I flee from your presence?
If I go up to the heavens, you are there;
  if I make my bed in the depths, you are there.
If I rise on the wings of the dawn,
  if I settle on the far side of the sea,
even there your hand will guide me,
  your right hand will hold me fast.
If I say, "Surely the darkness will hide me
  and the light become night around me,"
even the darkness will not be dark to you;
  the night will shine like the day,
  for darkness is as light to you.

For you created my inmost being;
  you knit me together in my mother's womb.
I praise you because I am fearfully and wonderfully made;
  your works are wonderful,
  I know that full well.
My frame was not hidden from you
  when I was made in the secret place,
  when I was woven together in the depths of the earth.
Your eyes saw my unformed body;
  all the days ordained for me were written in your book
  before one of them came to be.
                                                    Psalm 139:1-16

To recap, the Lord our God is the only God. He is one of a kind. He has amazing, awe-inspiring powers that we have heard about and have even experienced. He is the Creator of our world. He set the earth in motion and still controls it today — the sea, the wind, and the oceans.

The Lord once asked Job,
"Where were you when I laid the foundations of the earth?
  Tell me, if you know so much.
Who determined its dimensions

and stretched out the surveying line?
What supports its foundations,
* and who laid its cornerstone*
as the morning stars sang together
* and all the angels shouted for joy?*

"Who kept the sea inside its boundaries
* as it burst from the womb,*
and as I clothed it with clouds
* and wrapped it in thick darkness?*
For I locked it behind barred gates,
* limiting its shores.*
I said, 'This far and no farther will you come.
* Here your proud waves must stop!'*
"Have you ever commanded the morning to appear
* and caused the dawn to rise in the east?"*

Job 38:4-12 NLT

I know Job must have been in awe. These men of the past understood and appreciated the power and magnificence of God. Today, because our knowledge has increased, we think more of ourselves and appreciate God less. He is still doing marvelous and wondrous things every day, but now we take these things for granted. We have become our own gods. We call the Bible fairy tales and consider it foolish to believe the Bible and the God of the Bible. The apostle Paul wrote about this.

The message of the cross is foolishness to those who are perishing, but to us who are being saved it is the power of God. For it is written:
* "I will destroy the wisdom of the wise;*
* the intelligence of the intelligent I will frustrate."*

1 Corinthians 1:18-19

He later explained it further.

No one knows the thoughts of God except the Spirit of God. What we have received is not the spirit of the world, but the Spirit who is from God, so that we may understand what God has freely given us. This is what we speak, not in words taught us by human wisdom but in words taught by the Spirit, explaining spiritual realities with Spirit-taught

words. The person without the Spirit does not accept the things that come from the Spirit of God but considers them foolishness and cannot understand them because they are discerned only through the Spirit.
1 Corinthians 2:11-14

Therefore, it is necessary to have the Spirit of God to understand about my God, the Lord. It is the Spirit of God who communicates these wondrous things to us and helps us understand so that we can believe and get to know God, our Heavenly Father.

It is beyond the ability of any man to understand the things of God without the help of the Spirit of God. God has provided a way to communicate spiritual things with us. It is not for him, because he already sees and knows all. Even with all the noise and global chatter, God can hear a baby cry — as with Hagar and her child in the desert.

God heard the boy crying, and the angel of God called to Hagar from heaven and said to her, "What is the matter, Hagar? Do not be afraid; God has heard the boy crying as he lies there."
Genesis 21:17

The most important thing that makes God great is that he is the Creator of this earth and all in it. Also, when we look at the amazing details that are involved in making our bodies work so efficiently, it speaks to God's greatness. When we ponder on what it took to create the sun and the moon and to place the earth at just the right distance to keep us warm and give us light without destroying us, we should be in awe of this amazingly awe-inspiring God. When we look around at all the beautiful trees that were created to hold the oxygen we need to survive, we can truly appreciate his wisdom and know that we are in the presence of a supreme, unmatched intelligence.

We ought to honor and worship this God. To think that He wants to have a relationship with what he has created, and to come and live among us, is mind-boggling. We should be honored to make room for him in our lives.

There is much more to this world that we live in than meets the eyes. There is another spirit world that is all around us, yet we live as though we are in a vacuum, and we are all that matters and all that exists. Our God, the Lord, can also open our eyes to see more than the natural eye can see.

One example in the Bible is when God showed Hagar a well of water that she could not see with her natural eyes.

Then God opened her eyes and she saw a well of water. So, she went and filled the skin with water and gave the boy a drink.

Genesis 21:19

Another example is when the prophet Elisha prayed that God would open his servant's eyes so that he could see what Elisha saw.

And Elisha prayed, "Open his eyes, Lord, so that he may see." Then the Lord opened the servant's eyes, and he looked and saw the hills full of horses and chariots of fire all around Elisha.

2 Kings 6:17

And God opened the eyes of Balaam to see an angel.

Then the Lord opened Balaam's eyes, and he saw the angel of the Lord standing in the road with his sword drawn. So, he bowed low and fell face down.

Numbers 22:31

So, if we could all see everything that is around us, we would probably all believe. But this is reserved for the insiders, or those who choose to believe God. Also, if we knew that there were other spirits watching all that we do, it might make a difference in how we lived. Paul spoke of that.

Therefore, since we are surrounded by such a great cloud of witnesses, let us throw off everything that hinders and the sin that so easily entangles. And let us run with perseverance the race marked out for us.

Hebrews 12:1

We could not know about God unless he had revealed himself to us. He is:

...the Creator of the heavens, who stretches them out,
   who spreads out the earth with all that springs from it,
   who gives breath to its people,
   and life to those who walk on it.

Isaiah 42:5

For these reasons, I really want you to meet my God. You see, he is truly an awesome God, and he promises to take care of those who love him.

"For I know the plans I have for you," declares the Lord, "plans to prosper you and not to harm you, plans to give you hope and a future. Then you will call on me and come and pray to me, and I will listen to you. You will seek me and find me when you seek me with all your heart."

Jeremiah 29:11-13

3
His Dwelling Place — He Owns It All

"To the Lord your God belong the heavens, even the highest heavens, the earth and everything in it."

Deuteronomy 10:14

My God, the Lord, asked Jeremiah,

"Who can hide in secret places so that I cannot see them? ...Do not I fill heaven and earth?"

Jeremiah 23:24

God fills the heaven and the earth, so that is why he is everywhere at the same time, which speaks of his omnipresence. However, not only does he occupy all of heaven and earth, but he also owns all of it (read again, Deuteronomy 10:14). So how do we build a temple for God?

David had this great idea to build a Temple for God. God had given Israel the Promised Land as promised, and David had built a huge palace for himself. Now he wanted to show his appreciation for God by building him a Temple.

The symbols of God's presence had been stored away in an Ark inside the Tabernacle, which was like a portable temple. Now David wanted to build a decent resting place for these emblems, which represented God's presence and reminded them of how he led them through the wilderness day and night, to deliver to them the Promised Land. David felt that building his Temple was the least they could do.

David was excited by the idea, but when he spoke to the prophet Nathan about his plans, God said, "Thanks, but no thanks." We can read about it in 2 Samuel 7.

To paraphrase, that night God told the prophet Nathan to tell David,

"So, you want to build me a house? I have not lived in a house since I

brought your people out of Egypt. I have been moving around in a tent, but I have never complained or asked any of the rulers of Israel to build me a house of cedar. But you, David, I took you from tending sheep and made you ruler over my people. I have been with you and fought your battles for you. Now, I am going to make your name great among the greatest of men. I will provide for you and your people and will give you rest from your enemies. But as for this house, I am the one who will build you a house. Long after you are dead and gone, I will raise up one of your offspring to succeed you. He will be your own flesh and blood, and I will establish His kingdom. He is the one who will build a house for my Name, and I will establish the throne of his kingdom forever. I will be His father and he will be my Son. I will never take away my love from him as I did with Saul. Your house and your kingdom will endure forever before me."

2 Samuel 7:5-16

Most people, including David, thought God was referring to Solomon as the son who would build the Temple. However, if we examine God's message carefully, we realize God was really trying to share with David the exciting message about the future kingdom. God said that long after David had died, he would raise up a Son to build the Temple, but David set up his son Solomon to build the Temple before he died. God said that this offspring of David would be his Son as well, but Solomon was never called God's son. God also said that the Son's throne would last forever, and we all know that Solomon's throne did not last forever.

This is not to say that God did not appreciate David building a house for him, but God knew how unstable that house would be. Every time an enemy threatened, the people would take the gold from the Temple and give it to the enemy. Another king would offer sacrifices to other gods in Solomon's Temple. Enemies would burn it down, and God did not want to live in a place like that. However, the temple that Jesus would build would be a place where God could truly put up his feet. He told Ezekiel about it. As Ezekiel received a tour of the future temple, he heard the Lord speaking to him.

The Lord said to me, "Son of man, this is the place of my throne and the place where I will rest my feet. I will live here forever among the people of Israel."

Ezekiel 43:7NLT

This God, my Father, the Lord, owns and fills the heavens and the earth and can live wherever he chooses, but his favorite spot in all this world seems to be Mount Zion.

For the Lord has chosen Zion,
  he has desired it for his dwelling, saying,
"This is my resting place for ever and ever;
  here I will sit enthroned, for I have desired it.

Psalm 132:13-14

Zion seems to refer to that range of mountains from Bethel to Jerusalem. It encompasses the fortress near Jerusalem that was called the city of David. Zion is most often called Mount Zion.

Beautiful in its loftiness,
  the joy of the whole earth,
like the heights of Zaphon is Mount Zion,
  the city of the Great King.

Psalm 48:2

The whole area, including Jerusalem, is referred to as Zion. It is the land where most of the Bible took place. It is where the Lord met with Moses and wrestled with Jacob.

Bethel, also known as Luz, is at the entrance to the Promised Land or Canaan, now Israel. When Abraham set out to follow God, one of the first stops he made was between Bethel and Ai. He built an altar there to God and called on the name of the Lord. On his entrance into Canaan, God, the Lord, revealed to Abraham that this was the land he would give to his offspring (Genesis 12:6-8).

When Jacob was running away from his brother Esau after deceptively taking his blessing, his first stop was also at Bethel. There he had an encounter with God that left him with the impression that this place was the "gate of heaven," and "the house of God."

When Jacob awoke from his sleep, he thought, "Surely the Lord is in this place, and I was not aware of it." He was afraid and said, "How awesome is this place! This is none other than the house of God; this is the gate of heaven."

Genesis 28:16-17

Jacob renamed the place Bethel. Twice Jacob had encounters at that place. When Jacob returned home, God told him to settle at Bethel and build an altar there to the Lord.

> *Then God said to Jacob, "Go up to Bethel and settle there, and build an altar there to God, who appeared to you when you were fleeing from your brother Esau."*

Genesis 35:1

However, Jacob did not remain at Bethel but went back to live where his father Isaac had lived (Genesis 37:1). If Jacob had remained at Bethel, perhaps his offspring would not have spent four hundred years in slavery in Egypt. Perhaps they could have avoided that long, painful journey back to the Promised Land. Disobedience comes with a price. When Jacob moved from Bethel, things started to go downhill. Rachel died in childbirth (Genesis 35:16-18) and his father Isaac died as well.

Many years later, when the Israelites returned to claim the land around Bethel, King Jeroboam erected high places to false gods there. That was an abomination, to desecrate a holy place that God had chosen for his people. Bethel was a place God had loved and chosen for both Abraham and Jacob. I would not be surprised if it plays a big part in the future kingdom.

> *"But will God really dwell on earth with humans? The heavens, even the highest heavens, cannot contain you."*

2 Chronicles 6:18

Even after Solomon had built a most royal Temple unto God, he could not understand God's ability to dwell among his people on earth. At the dedication of the Temple, he basically said that the Temple was just symbolic. He did not expect God to dwell there, but it would be a place that represented a connection point between God and his people. It would be a place where God's people would come to experience the presence of their God. It would be a meeting place for their Feast Days and Holy Days.

Although God gave King Solomon greater wisdom than most men, Solomon later built other temples to the gods of his pagan wives. This could not have been pleasing to the Lord.

The Lord became angry with Solomon because his heart had turned away from the Lord, the God of Israel, who had appeared to him twice.
1 Kings 11:9

However, God loved Solomon even though he knew in advance that he would do this in the future.

My Heavenly Father cares for the Land of Israel. Just as he chose Israel, the people, as his own, he has also chosen the Land as well.

It is a land the Lord your God cares for; the eyes of the Lord your God are continually on it from the beginning of the year to its end.
Deuteronomy 11:12

One day, my God, the Lord, will bring his kingdom to earth and reign from Jerusalem forever. Throughout the Bible, he has told us about that day. John saw it.

And I heard a loud voice from the throne saying, "Look! God's dwelling place is now among the people, and he will dwell with them. They will be his people, and God himself will be with them and be their God.
Revelation 21:3

The Lord himself told Micah about this.

Then I, the Lord, will rule from Jerusalem as their king forever.
Micah 4:7 NLT

The prophet Zechariah also spoke of it.

"Sing and rejoice, O daughter of Zion! For behold, I am coming and I will dwell in your midst," says the Lord. "Many nations shall be joined to the Lord in that day, and they shall become My people. And I will dwell in your midst. Then you will know that the Lord of hosts has sent Me to you.
Zechariah 2:10-11 NKJV

Creator living in his creation! What an amazing concept!
He owns it all. He told Israel,

I have no need of a bull from your stall
*   or of goats from your pens,*
for every animal of the forest is mine,

and the cattle on a thousand hills.
I know every bird in the mountains,
* and the insects in the fields are mine.*
If I were hungry I would not tell you,
* for the world is mine, and all that is in it."*

Psalm 50:9-12

Yes, God owns it all. He does not need anything from us. However, he does want a relationship with us. He could live anywhere, but he desires to live among his people on Mount Zion.

When God does come to live and reign from Jerusalem, we will learn of his true power and authority. The prophet Zechariah told us that the wealth of all the nations shall be transferred to the kingdom of God.

And the wealth of all the surrounding nations
Shall be gathered together:
Gold, silver, and apparel in great abundance.

Zechariah 14:14 NKJV

Again, this will not be for God himself, because he already owns it; but it will be to minister to those who have just survived the massive earthquake, nuclear disaster, and world war in Jerusalem. Read about it in Zechariah 14. My God and Heavenly Father, the Lord, does not just have command over the physical world but also over the spiritual world. On that Day, which we refer to as the Day of the Lord or Judgment Day, he will first bind the evil one for one thousand years.

Then I saw an angel coming down from heaven, having the key to the bottomless pit and a great chain in his hand. He laid hold of the dragon, that serpent of old, who is the Devil and Satan, and bound him for a thousand years; and he cast him into the bottomless pit, and shut him up, and set a seal on him, so that he should deceive the nations no more till the thousand years were finished.

Revelation 20:1-3

You are probably thinking, "If God has this power, then why hasn't he done it before?" The fact is, he has already given us the power to cast out devils. Jesus told His disciples,

And as you go, preach, saying, "The kingdom of heaven is at hand." Heal the sick, cleanse the lepers, raise the dead, cast out demons. Freely you have received, freely give.

Matthew 10:7-8 NKJV

In fact, from the beginning, my God, the Lord, gave us dominion and set us up to rule everything that moves.

Then God blessed them, and God said to them, "Be fruitful and multiply; fill the earth and subdue it; have dominion over the fish of the sea, over the birds of the air, and over every living thing that moves on the earth."

Genesis 1:28 NKJV

We never did truly understand what it meant to have dominion or rule, so God sent his Son to show us how to live. Jesus went about healing the sick, casting out demons, raising the dead, and speaking to storms. Before Jesus left, He told His disciples,

These signs will follow those who believe: In My name they will cast out demons; they will speak with new tongues; they will take up serpents; and if they drink anything deadly, it will by no means hurt them; they will lay hands on the sick, and they will recover."

Mark 16:17-18 NKJV

We already have the authority over many things, yet we wait for God to do everything for us. We suffer needlessly and cannot understand why we have so many adversities. You see, God wants to use these experiences to grow our faith in him and to equip us for life. We were made in his image, even though we do not act like it. We blame God for all the evil in the world, but he has already equipped us to handle it. We can do all things through faith in him. His plan was for us to have dominion and handle all these issues. Without faith, we cannot please him. Paul wrote about it.

Without faith it is impossible to please God.

Hebrews 11:6

We live in a world where slavery is more rampant than at any other time, where evil and poverty are prevalent. This is not God's fault. He has equipped us to handle all of this, but we sit back and wait for him to handle it. We have failed miserably, and that is why one day, on the Day of the Lord, he is coming down here to fix all this himself. He will live and reign on earth from Jerusalem and show us how to live in peace and harmony. When the Lord comes to live on earth, he will do what we should have done. He will bind the devil and make life a peaceful and pleasant experience for all.

> *Rejoice greatly, Daughter Zion!*
> *Shout, Daughter Jerusalem!*
> *See, your king comes to you,*
> *righteous and victorious,*
> *lowly and riding on a donkey,*
> *on a colt, the foal of a donkey.*
> *I will take away the chariots from Ephraim*
> *and the warhorses from Jerusalem,*
> *and the battle bow will be broken.*
> *He will proclaim peace to the nations.*
> *His rule will extend from sea to sea*
> *and from the River to the ends of the earth.*
>
> *Zechariah 9:9-10*

4
He Has Feelings Too

For God so loved the world that He gave His one and only Son, that whoever believes in him shall not perish but have eternal life.

John 3:16

My God, the Lord, is Master Creator of the Universe and the Lord of Heaven's Armies, yet he openly displays his emotions and his love for us, his created beings. God, our Heavenly Father, is a very passionate God. He is not ashamed to say, "I love you."

He chose the people of Israel to demonstrate his love. He loves these descendants of Abraham and spoke tenderly to them through Isaiah.

But now, thus says the Lord, who created you, O Jacob,
And He who formed you, O Israel:
"Fear not, for I have redeemed you;
I have called you by your name;
You are Mine.
When you pass through the waters, I will be with you;
And through the rivers, they shall not overflow you. When you walk
through the fire, you shall not be burned,
Nor shall the flame scorch you.
For I am the Lord your God,
The Holy One of Israel, your Savior;
I gave Egypt for your ransom,
Ethiopia and Seba in your place.
Since you were precious in My sight,
You have been honored,
And I have loved you;
Therefore, I will give men for you,
And people for your life.

Fear not, for I am with you."

Isaiah 43:1-5 NKJV

God speaks the love language. However, this beloved nation did not always return his love. They were not faithful. They wanted to worship false gods like their neighbors. Yet, this all-powerful God, who could wipe them out with a thought, continued in this same message in Isaiah 43 to gently plead with them about returning his love. He said,

"But you have not called upon Me, O Jacob;
And you have been weary of Me, O Israel.
You have not brought Me the sheep for your burnt offerings,
Nor have you honored Me with your sacrifices.
I have not caused you to serve with grain offerings,
Nor wearied you with incense.
You have bought Me no sweet cane with money,
Nor have you satisfied Me with the fat of your sacrifices;
But you have burdened Me with your sins,
You have wearied Me with your iniquities.
I, even I, am He who blots out your transgressions for My own sake;
And I will not remember your sins.
Put Me in remembrance;
Let us contend together;
State your case, that you may be acquitted."

Isaiah 43:22-26 NKJV

Time after time, he forgave them "for his own sake." If it was left up to us to seek the Lord, we would be hopeless; so, he made the first move. He would usually make a conscious effort to forgive us and renew the relationship. John said,

We love because He first loved us.

1 John 4:19

My God, the Lord, is so wonderful! He is a lover. In fact, John went one step further and said that God is love. He said,

Whoever does not love does not know God, because God is love.

1 John 4:8

We learn in John 3:16 that this same God, who loves so tenderly, was even willing to sacrifice his own Son for a people who would not even acknowledge that he existed.

For God so loved the world that He gave His one and only Son, that whoever believes in him shall not perish but have eternal life.

John 3:16

Mankind has looked at this precious, divine display of affection and arrived at the wrong impression of God. They ask, "How can such a loving God allow such atrocious disasters to happen?" They have missed the point that we also have a part to play in this love affair. Even though God has and will always go above and beyond to show his love, he expects us to reciprocate. You see, he made a covenant of love with his people Israel. It is like marriage vows. He told them,

Love the Lord your God with all your heart and with all your soul and with all your strength.

Deuteronomy 6:5

This covenant of love came with blessings for faithfulness and curses for unfaithfulness. He promised them:

If you fully obey the Lord your God and carefully follow all his commands I give you today, the Lord your God will set you high above all the nations on earth. All these blessings will come on you and accompany you if you obey the Lord your God:

You will be blessed in the city and blessed in the country.

The fruit of your womb will be blessed, and the crops of your land and the young of your livestock—the calves of your herds and the lambs of your flocks.

Your basket and your kneading trough will be blessed.

You will be blessed when you come in and blessed when you go out.

The Lord will grant that the enemies who rise up against you will be defeated before you. They will come at you from one direction but flee from you in seven.

The Lord will send a blessing on your barns and on everything you put your hand to. The Lord your God will bless you in the land he is giving you.

The Lord will establish you as his holy people, as he promised you on oath, if you keep the commands of the Lord your God and walk in obedience to him. Then all the peoples on earth will see that you are called by the name of the Lord, and they will fear you. The Lord will grant you abundant prosperity—in the fruit of your womb, the young of your livestock and the crops of your ground—in the land he swore to your ancestors to give you.

The Lord will open the heavens, the storehouse of his bounty, to send rain on your land in season and to bless all the work of your hands. You will lend to many nations but will borrow from none. The Lord will make you the head, not the tail. If you pay attention to the commands of the Lord your God that I give you this day and carefully follow them, you will always be at the top, never at the bottom. Do not turn aside from any of the commands I give you today, to the right or to the left, following other gods and serving them.

Deuteronomy 28:1-14

What else could anyone want? The Creator of our world loves you and has promised to give you every good thing that there is if you are faithful to him. It does not make any sense that anyone would turn down that offer. However, Israel chose to give up being special to be like the other nations. They wanted what they could not have, just like Adam and Eve. They chose the forbidden fruit. They had to suffer the consequences for this decision.

The curses that came with this covenant of love were far more numerous than the blessings. They were told:

However, if you do not obey the Lord your God and do not carefully follow all his commands and decrees I am giving you today, all these curses will come on you and overtake you:

You will be cursed in the city and cursed in the country.

Your basket and your kneading trough will be cursed.

The fruit of your womb will be cursed, and the crops of your land, and the calves of your herds and the lambs of your flocks.

You will be cursed when you come in and cursed when you go out.
The Lord will send on you curses, confusion and rebuke in everything
you put your hand to, until you are destroyed and come to sudden
ruin because of the evil you have done in forsaking him. The Lord will
plague you with diseases until he has destroyed you from the land you
are entering to possess. The Lord will strike you with wasting disease,
with fever and inflammation, with scorching heat and drought, with
blight and mildew, which will plague you until you perish. The sky
over your head will be bronze, the ground beneath you iron. The Lord
will turn the rain of your country into dust and powder; it will come
down from the skies until you are destroyed.

The Lord will cause you to be defeated before your enemies. You will
come at them from one direction but flee from them in seven, and
you will become a thing of horror to all the kingdoms on earth. Your
carcasses will be food for all the birds and the wild animals, and there
will be no one to frighten them away. The Lord will afflict you with the
boils of Egypt and with tumors, festering sores and the itch, from which
you cannot be cured. The Lord will afflict you with madness, blindness
and confusion of mind. At midday you will grope about like a blind
person in the dark. You will be unsuccessful in everything you do; day
after day you will be oppressed and robbed, with no one to rescue you.
You will be pledged to be married to a woman, but another will take
her and rape her. You will build a house, but you will not live in it.
                                            Deuteronomy 28:15-30

The list of curses went on and on, including some of the most horrible
things that one can imagine. The Lord even told them that with the same
intensity that he blessed them, he would seek to destroy them.

Just as it pleased the Lord to make you prosper and increase in number,
so it will please him to ruin and destroy you.
                                            Deuteronomy 28:63

There is a reason for all this madness and misfortune that we encounter.
We rejected the Lord's loving, outstretched hand and chose the unthinkable

alternative, forgetting that it is a terrible thing to fall under the fire of God's anger. He is a very jealous God.

Do not follow other gods, the gods of the peoples around you; for the Lord your God, who is among you, is a jealous God and his anger will burn against you, and he will destroy you from the face of the land.

Deuteronomy 6:14-15

We hear so much about God's love, but that is only half of the story. We ought to tell as well about God's jealousy. Not knowing could be extremely devastating.

Moses warned them:

Do not worship any other god, for the Lord, whose name is Jealous, is a jealous God.

Exodus 34:14

Joshua warned them:

Joshua said to the people, "You are not able to serve the Lord. He is a holy God; he is a jealous God. He will not forgive your rebellion and your sins. If you forsake the Lord and serve foreign gods, he will turn and bring disaster on you and make an end of you, after he has been good to you."

Joshua 24:19-20

The Lord Himself told them:

You shall not bow down to them or worship them; for I, the Lord your God, am a jealous God, punishing the children for the sin of the parents to the third and fourth generation of those who hate me.

Deuteronomy 5:9

Yes, God's jealousy is as real as his love. A poet once wrote, "The rules of fair play do not apply in love and war." But with God, he is as fair as he could be. He forewarns about the consequence of being unfaithful. He pleads…he is patient and waits for us to repent. He is also willing to forgive and forget.

We also need to tell about God's willingness to forgive. He promised Solomon,

"When I shut up the heavens so that there is no rain, or command locusts to devour the land or send a plague among my people, if my people, who are called by my name, will humble themselves and pray and seek my face and turn from their wicked ways, then I will hear from heaven, and I will forgive their sin and will heal their land."

2 Chronicles 7:13-14

No one ever needed to experience the curses of the covenant of love, because our Lord is so generous. He provided a way to be forgiven if we choose to repent. In the Old Testament, it was with the guilt offering.

With the ram of the guilt offering the priest is to make atonement for him before the Lord for the sin he has committed, and his sin will be forgiven.

Leviticus 19:22

In the New Testament, it is with the blood that Jesus shed for our sins. Jesus told the disciples,

"This is my blood of the covenant, which is poured out for many for the forgiveness of sins."

Matthew 26:28

We only need to read the story of the Israelites and of their up-and-down relationship with their God to see evidence of the Lord's jealousy and anger. They suffered much because they were unfaithful to Him. Also, in the days of Noah, he destroyed the whole human race except for Noah and his family. There were times when He killed tens of thousands of his own people in a day. He allowed over six million to be killed in the Holocaust. So why should it surprise us when other atrocities happen? We have a God who loves passionately, and we need to take that covenant of love more seriously. The Israelites were told:

These commandments that I give you today are to be on your hearts. Impress them on your children. Talk about them when you sit at home and when you walk along the road, when you lie down and when you get up. Tie them as symbols on your hands and bind them on your foreheads. Write them on the doorframes of your houses and on your gates.

Deuteronomy 6:6-9

Our God's Word should always be taken seriously. We should not take his love for granted. It is our most valuable possession, because without his love we are nothing.

If you ever forget the Lord your God and follow other gods and worship and bow down to them, I testify against you today that you will surely be destroyed. Like the nations the Lord destroyed before you, so you will be destroyed for not obeying the Lord your God.

Deuteronomy 8:19-20

Moses tried to explain to them what an honor it was and is to be loved by the Lord.

To the Lord your God belong the heavens, even the highest heavens, the earth and everything in it. Yet the Lord set his affection on your ancestors and loved them, and he chose you, their descendants, above all the nations—as it is today. Circumcise your hearts, therefore, and do not be stiff-necked any longer. For the Lord your God is God of gods and Lord of lords, the great God, mighty and awesome, who shows no partiality and accepts no bribes.

Deuteronomy 10:14-17

We do not have to worry that God will ever take his love from us if we are faithful. Our God is faithful and will always keep his Word in this covenant of love, in blessing or in cursing, and even when we sin and return to him and seek him.

Know therefore that the Lord your God is God; he is the faithful God, keeping his covenant of love to a thousand generations of those who love him and keep his commandments.

Deuteronomy 7:9

We should not take our God's love for granted though. We tend to think of love as an equalizer and do not understand that even though God loves us, we can never be his equal. He still demands our respect.

In Isaiah 14, we are told that Lucifer once thought that he could be like God, and he was thrown out of heaven for that. We should never consider ourselves equal with God. Paul spoke about this. He asked,

But who are you, a human being, to talk back to God? "Shall what is
formed say to the one who formed it, 'Why did you make me like this?'"
                                                                Romans 9:20

We do not get to tell God how he should act. He is not our equal. Job
learned that lesson and said,

"Naked I came from my mother's womb,
And naked shall I return there.
The Lord gave, and the Lord has taken away;
Blessed be the name of the Lord."

                                                                Job 1:21 NKJV

God allowed Job to be tested to prove that he would still trust him in
adversity. Job said,

"He knows the way that I take;
when He has tested me, I will come forth as gold."

                                                                Job 23:10

Sometimes it is necessary for God to allow tests to humble us and
to perfect us. It does not mean that he does not love us. We just need to
remain humble and respectful and remember that he is God. We need to
keep a healthy respect in our relationship with him and not begin to treat
him as our equal. Moses reminded the Israelites,

Remember how the Lord your God led you all the way in the wilderness
these forty years, to humble and test you in order to know what was in
your heart, whether or not you would keep his commands.

                                                                Deuteronomy 8:2

Even when we cannot understand his actions or the things he allows,
we ought to trust him, because he is the Creator and can see the bigger
picture. It will all work out for our good. His testing does not always feel
like love, but he rewards our faithfulness. Job got back more than he had
lost, and the Israelites were eventually led into the Land God had promised
them.

God's chosen people, whom my God, the Lord, loves, needed
correction often. They took his love for granted, and were, at times, very
unappreciative. For instance, when they were in Egypt and worshiping

the Egyptian gods, God still remembered his promise to Abraham and was excited to set them free and take them to the Promised Land. He sent Moses to tell them about it.

> *'Therefore, say to the Israelites: 'I am the Lord, and I will bring you out from under the yoke of the Egyptians. I will free you from being slaves to them, and I will redeem you with an outstretched arm and with mighty acts of judgment. I will take you as my own people, and I will be your God. Then you will know that I am the Lord your God, who brought you out from under the yoke of the Egyptians. And I will bring you to the land I swore with uplifted hand to give to Abraham, to Isaac and to Jacob. I will give it to you as a possession. I am the Lord.''*

> *Moses reported this to the Israelites, but they did not listen to him because of their discouragement and harsh labor.*
>
> *Exodus 6:6-9*

They did not show any appreciation for how God was making plans to change their lives, nor for the love that was causing God to overlook their sins and save them anyway.

Another shocking example of their ingratitude was when God caused them to be taken into exile by the Babylonians because they were once again serving other gods. However, he left a remnant in Jerusalem to occupy the city until the others came back. You would think they would appreciate that, but instead, they decided to move back to Egypt, where God had miraculously freed them from slavery. When Jeremiah tried to talk them out of going there, they were downright disrespectful to God. They talked to him as though he was their equal.

> *Then all the men who knew that their wives were burning incense to other gods, along with all the women who were present—a large assembly—and all the people living in Lower and Upper Egypt, said to Jeremiah, "We will not listen to the message you have spoken to us in the name of the Lord! We will certainly do everything we said we would: We will burn incense to the Queen of Heaven and will pour out drink offerings to her just as we and our ancestors, our kings and our officials did in the towns of Judah and in the streets of Jerusalem. At that time, we had plenty of food and were well off and suffered*

no harm. But ever since we stopped burning incense to the Queen of Heaven and pouring out drink offerings to her, we have had nothing and have been perishing by sword and famine."

Jeremiah 44:15-18

Can you believe that they had the nerve to speak to my God, the Lord, in this manner? They must have had a death wish. It is detrimental to defy my God and to snub his love. Yet, we do it today as well.

God is hurt by our contempt. He hears our conversations and is often offended by them. He spoke of this in Malachi 3.

"You have said terrible things about me," says the Lord.

"But you say, 'What do you mean? What have we said against you?'

"You have said, 'What's the use of serving God? What have we gained by obeying his commands or by trying to show the Lord of Heaven's Armies that we are sorry for our sins?

From now on we will call the arrogant blessed. For those who do evil get rich, and those who dare God to punish them suffer no harm.'"

Malachi 3:13-15 NLT

We obviously do not think that my God can hear us. We think of him as being far up in heaven and not interested in what we say. My God, the Lord, hears our conversations and records them. Malachi told us about it.

Then those who feared the Lord spoke with each other, and the Lord listened to what they said. In his presence, a scroll of remembrance was written to record the names of those who feared him and always thought about the honor of his name.

"They will be my people," says the Lord of Heaven's Armies. "On the day when I act in judgment, they will be my own special treasure. I will spare them as a father spares an obedient child. Then you will again see the difference between the righteous and the wicked, between those who serve God and those who do not."

Malachi 3:16-18 NLT

Even though my God and my Father had some difficulty choosing a people who would return his love fully, he found some individuals who understood his love and appreciated it. They were not perfect, but he loved them just the same. Let us look at some of those people and what God said about them.

Noah

When God decided to destroy the wicked people of the world, he found that Noah was faithful and decided to share his plans with him. It had never rained before, but God told Noah that it would rain so much that it would cause a disastrous flood. He instructed Noah to build an Ark, where Noah and his family could be protected from the flood. Noah was faithful to do as God commanded him, even when it did not seem to make sense and even though it took 120 years to happen as God promised. Here is what was said about him:

> *But Noah found favor in the eyes of the Lord...Noah was a righteous man, blameless among the people of his time, and he walked faithfully with God.*
>
> *Genesis 6:8-9*

Abraham

Abraham has been referred to as the Father of our faith. Paul wrote much about his faith.

> *By faith Abraham obeyed when he was called to go out to the place which he would receive as an inheritance. And he went out, not knowing where he was going.*
>
> *Hebrews 11:8 NKJV*

> *By faith Abraham, when he was tested, offered up Isaac, and he who had received the promises offered up his only begotten son.*
>
> *Hebrews 11:17 NKJV*

James told us that he was called the friend of God.

> *And the Scripture was fulfilled which says, "Abraham believed God, and it was accounted to him for righteousness." And he was called the friend of God.*

James 2:23 NKJV

When God was getting ready to destroy Sodom and Gomorrah, he decided to share it with Abraham.

> *And the Lord said, "Shall I hide from Abraham what I am doing, since Abraham shall surely become a great and mighty nation, and all the nations of the earth shall be blessed in him? For I have known him, in order that he may command his children and his household after him, that they keep the way of the Lord, to do righteousness and justice, that the Lord may bring to Abraham what He has spoken to him." And the Lord said, "Because the outcry against Sodom and Gomorrah is great, and because their sin is very grave, I will go down now and see whether they have done altogether according to the outcry against it that has come to Me; and if not, I will know."*
>
> *Then the men turned away from there and went toward Sodom, but Abraham still stood before the Lord.*
>
> *Genesis 18:17-22 NKJV*

Abraham's humility in that encounter was quite becoming. He showed great respect for the Lord.

> *Then Abraham answered and said, "Indeed now, I who am but dust and ashes have taken it upon myself to speak to the Lord."*
>
> *Genesis 18:27 NKJV*

Levi

Levi was one of Jacob's sons, a perceived rebel, and the grandfather of Moses. God said about him,

> *"And you will know that I have sent you this warning so that my covenant with Levi may continue," says the Lord Almighty. "My covenant was with him, a covenant of life and peace, and I gave them to him; this called for reverence and he revered me and stood in awe of my name. True instruction was in his mouth and nothing false was found on his lips. He walked with me in peace and uprightness and turned many from sin."*
>
> *Malachi 2:4-6*

Even Jacob, his father, did not understand him. He thought that he was too violent and did not give him much of a blessing when he was blessing his sons; but God knew him, understood him, and made a covenant with him. God chose his offspring to be priests unto him. The Levites served God in the Temple for many generations. God also chose his grandsons, Moses and Aaron, to lead his people.

David

During David's younger life, he spent a lot of time on his own, tending sheep, and got to know the Lord very well. Here is what God said about him:

> "After removing Saul, he made David their king. God testified concerning him: 'I have found David son of Jesse, a man after my own heart; he will do everything I want him to do.'"
>
> *Acts 13:22*

David was by no means perfect. He had his sinful episodes. He was subject to the sinful nature like us all, but what set him apart was his love and respect for the Lord. When he sinned, he would genuinely repent and seek God with all his heart. Like God, he was very passionate. We have his psalms as evidence of that. He was not ashamed to seek God openly. When he danced before God with all his might during the transport of the Ark to Jerusalem, his wife thought it was vulgar and not becoming of a king.

> So David said to Michal, "It was before the Lord, who chose me instead of your father and all his house, to appoint me ruler over the people of the Lord, over Israel. Therefore, I will play music before the Lord. And I will be even more undignified than this and will be humble in my own sight."
>
> *2 Samuel 6:21-22 NKJV*

Jacob

God loved Jacob, the grandson of Abraham. He appeared to him twice, wrestled with him, and changed his name. God told Malachi,

> "Was not Esau Jacob's brother? ...Yet I have loved Jacob, but Esau I have hated."
>
> *Malachi 1:2-3*

That does not sound like something we would expect a righteous God to say. We hear sermons all the time that say God loves everyone, but God is also honest. Here are some of the things that could cause him to hate:

"For you are not a God who is pleased with wickedness;
with you, evil people are not welcome.
The arrogant cannot stand
in your presence.
You hate all who do wrong;
you destroy those who tell lies.
The bloodthirsty and deceitful
you, Lord, detest."

Psalm 5:4-6

"So I will come to put you on trial. I will be quick to testify against sorcerers, adulterers and perjurers, against those who defraud laborers of their wages, who oppress the widows and the fatherless, and deprive the foreigners among you of justice, but do not fear me," says the Lord Almighty.

Malachi 3:5

"God opposes the proud
but shows favor to the humble."

James 4:6

The Lord detests all the proud of heart.
Be sure of this: They will not go unpunished.

Proverbs 16:5

God most likely hated Esau because of his character and because he did not fear Him. Jacob, on the other hand, was faithful to his father-in-law, even when he switched the promised bride and caused him to work another seven years for the daughter he loved.

These are only a few of the men who returned God's love and were faithful to the Lord. There are many more. It boils down to this:

Blessed is the one
who does not walk in step with the wicked
or stand in the way that sinners take

or sit in the company of mockers,
but whose delight is in the law of the Lord,
 and who meditates on his law day and night.
That person is like a tree planted by streams of water,
 which yields its fruit in season
and whose leaf does not wither—
 whatever they do prospers.

Psalm 1:1-3

My God, the Lord, and my best friend knows my name. I know he loves me, and not only because he gave his only Son to die for my sins. He also sends little surprise blessings that are like love notes when I least expect them. He knows my favorite color. He blessed me with a car when I was not looking for one, and I did not even get to pick the color. It turned out to be my favorite color. It was no co-incidence. When he makes these beautiful gestures, I always know without a doubt who is behind it all. My love-note blessings are too numerous to tell here, but he wants to do the same for you. He asks that you,

> *Seek first his kingdom and his righteousness, and all these things will be given to you as well.*
>
>

Matthew 6:33

We also have a covenant of love with him, and he is still looking for an opportunity to bless us. If we reject his love, we will be cursed. However, he has provided a way out for us.

> *Christ has redeemed us from the curse of the law, having become a curse for us (for it is written, "Cursed is everyone who hangs on a tree").*
>
>

Galatians 3:13 NKJV

The Lord, our God, loves us. He wants to bless us and not curse us. He said, and is saying even now,

> *"For I know the plans I have for you," declares the Lord, "plans to prosper you and not to harm you, plans to give you hope and a future."*
>
>

Jeremiah 29:11

5
We Need Him More Than We Realize

Trust in the Lord with all your heart,
And lean not on your own understanding;
In all your ways acknowledge Him,
And He shall direct your paths.

Proverbs 3:5-6 NKJV

Abimelek and Phicol noticed the work of God in Abraham's life, and told him, "God is with you in everything you do" (Genesis 21:22). When we love God, we can take this quite literally. God is involved in everything we do. Whether we choose to acknowledge his involvement is another matter. Like puppets on a string, we can enact the will of God but deny the contact. The fact is, we need God's help more than we realize.

Sometimes we get frustrated when things do not go the way we want them to go, and we are not aware that God is saving us from things we cannot see. He sees where our desires can lead, and His intervention saves us from hurt. All we see is that our efforts are being frustrated, and we may even think God does not care. We ought to trust him more.

For instance, in 2 Kings 20, King Hezekiah of Judah was very ill and prayed for healing. Instead, God sent a message by Isaiah that he should get his house in order, because he was going to die. Hezekiah did what most of us would probably do. He cried unto God to give him more time. He should have just trusted God's decision. In retrospect, we can see now what God was trying to avoid.

God granted Hezekiah another fifteen years to live. During those fifteen years, Hezekiah's son, Manasseh, was born, and he turned out to be the worst king of all the kings of Judah, setting the nation on a downward spiral.

Manasseh offered sacrifices to false gods in the Temple that Solomon had built for the Lord. Also during those added years, Hezekiah had some visitors from Babylon, and he showed them all he had. Later, they came back and took it all to Babylon, including the people of Judah.

God was not being evil when he tried to cut Hezekiah's life short. He was trying to avoid those things he could see in the future. Hezekiah could not see the future, so he should have just trusted God.

When good things are happening to and around us, we tend to get happy and boastful, but in everything we ought to give thanks to our Heavenly Father, because he allows them to happen to and for us. Sometimes it involves his preparation far in advance to allow it to happen just right. Moses told the Israelites,

> *You may say to yourself, "My power and the strength of my hands have produced this wealth for me." But remember the Lord your God, for it is he who gives you the ability to produce wealth.*
>
> *Deuteronomy 8:17-18*

Joseph trusted God, and it brought him great success after many years of being led by God through some very difficult situations. When Joseph went from slave and prisoner to vice president of Egypt in one day, he did not claim that his wisdom got him that job. He understood that God had been working this out in his life ever since he was a child. As a child, God even gave him dreams to prepare him for this. He told his brothers, who had sold him into slavery,

> *"But as for you, you meant evil against me; but God meant it for good, in order to bring it about as it is this day, to save many people alive."*
>
> *Genesis 50:20 NKJV*

On rare occasions, he may give us a glimpse behind the scenes, so we can see what he is saving us from. When the Israelites got to the Promised Land, they may have wanted to eliminate all their enemies at once, so they could get a fresh start in the land their God had given them. However, God had a plan and a purpose for that plan. They were warned even before they got there.

> *Moreover, the Lord your God will send the hornet among them until even the survivors who hide from you have perished. Do not be terrified by them, for the Lord your God, who is among you, is a great and awesome God. The Lord your God will drive out those nations before*

you, little by little. You will not be allowed to eliminate them all at once, or the wild animals will multiply around you.

Deuteronomy 7.20-22

God thought of everything, and he can see what we cannot see; so, we just need to trust him. This is what Solomon meant when he admonished us to acknowledge God in all we do, and he will guide and direct us.

Trust in the Lord with all your heart
  and lean not on your own understanding;
In all your ways acknowledge Him,
  and He shall direct your paths.

Proverbs 3:5-6 NKJV

The Lord does not automatically guide everyone. If he did, we would all live in perfect harmony. When we trust and acknowledge him, he will direct our paths. He does not orchestrate the evil that is done in the world, but he can use it to push us in the direction we need to go.

The journey of the Israelites through the desert has a lot of lessons for us on how to trust God to lead us. In the beginning of their journey, God fought their battles for them or caused them to avoid battles. They felt they were prepared for battle. We read,

So God led the people around by the desert road toward the Red Sea. The Israelites went up out of Egypt ready for battle.

Exodus 13:18

However, it is interesting how even though the pursuing Egyptians were so close, God kept them at bay, until the Israelites had crossed the Red Sea.

Then the angel of God, who had been traveling in front of Israel's army, withdrew and went behind them. The pillar of cloud also moved from in front and stood behind them, coming between the armies of Egypt and Israel. Throughout the night the cloud brought darkness to the one side and light to the other side; so neither went near the other all night long.

Exodus 14:19-20

God was always there for them on that journey, leading them with visible emblems like a pillar of cloud or fire; but they continued to complain at the slightest discomfort, and it was hard for them to learn to trust him, to let go and let him lead. Moses reminded them,

> *Remember how the Lord your God led you all the way in the wilderness these forty years, to humble and test you in order to know what was in your heart, whether or not you would keep his commands. He humbled you, causing you to hunger and then feeding you with manna, which neither you nor your ancestors had known, to teach you that man does not live on bread alone but on every word that comes from the mouth of the Lord. Your clothes did not wear out and your feet did not swell during these forty years. Know then in your heart that as a man disciplines his son, so the Lord your God disciplines you.*
>
> *Deuteronomy 8:2-5*

Today, we can trust God to lead us in the same way he led the Israelites. He wants to fight our battles and provide for us in the same way, but we need to acknowledge him and trust him. Jesus also taught this sort of care-free living.

> *Then He said to His disciples, "Therefore I say to you, do not worry about your life, what you will eat; nor about the body, what you will put on. Life is more than food, and the body is more than clothing. Consider the ravens, for they neither sow nor reap, which have neither storehouse nor barn; and God feeds them. Of how much more value are you than the birds? And which of you by worrying can add one cubit to his stature? If you then are not able to do the least, why are you anxious for the rest? Consider the lilies, how they grow: they neither toil nor spin; and yet I say to you, even Solomon in all his glory was not arrayed like one of these. If then God so clothes the grass, which today is in the field and tomorrow is thrown into the oven, how much more will He clothe you, O you of little faith? And do not seek what you should eat or what you should drink, nor have an anxious mind. For all these things the nations of the world seek after, and your Father knows that you need these things. But seek the kingdom of God, and all these things shall be added to you.*
>
> *Luke 12:22-31 NKJV*

My God, the Lord, even designed our lives with our needs in mind. He knows that rest is important for us to function at peak capacity, so he designed the Sabbath to allow us to get our needed rest. Even God rested from his work, but we do not feel that we need to. The Sabbath is a gift from God, so why do we resist it? Obedience is better than sacrifice.

> *The seventh day is a sabbath to the Lord your God. On it you shall not do any work, neither you, nor your son or daughter, nor your male or female servant, nor your animals, nor any foreigner residing in your towns.*
>
> *Exodus 20:10*

We ignore God to our own detriment. He said that we do not prosper because of our own acts.

> *Then the Spirit of God came upon Zechariah son of Jehoiada the priest. He stood before the people and said, "This is what God says: Why do you disobey the Lord's commands and keep yourselves from prospering? You have abandoned the Lord, and now he has abandoned you!"*
>
> *2 Chronicles 24:20 NLT*

My God, the Lord says that there need be no poor among us. He has devised a plan for prosperity, and if we will do as he says, we will all prosper. God told his people,

> *"There should be no poor among you, for the Lord your God will greatly bless you in the land he is giving you as a special possession. You will receive this blessing if you are careful to obey all the commands of the Lord your God that I am giving you today. The Lord your God will bless you as He has promised. You will lend money to many nations but will never need to borrow. You will rule many nations, but they will not rule over you.*
>
> *"But if there are any poor Israelites in your towns when you arrive in the land the Lord your God is giving you, do not be hard-hearted or tightfisted toward them. Instead, be generous and lend them whatever they need."*
>
> *Deuteronomy 15:4-8 NLT*

Their God, the Lord, did bless them. He set up a social system for them to share their wealth with the poor neighbors, strangers, widows, and orphans. He intended to drive out poverty so that we should all have what we need. However, when we do not follow his plan, many suffer needlessly.

He also wants to heal us and keep us healthy.

He said, "If you listen carefully to the Lord your God and do what is right in his eyes, if you pay attention to his commands and keep all his decrees, I will not bring on you any of the diseases I brought on the Egyptians, for I am the Lord, who heals you."

Exodus 15:26

He will also fight our battles.

When you go into battle in your own land against an enemy who is oppressing you, sound a blast on the trumpets. Then you will be remembered by the Lord your God and rescued from your enemies.

Numbers 10:9

We may think that we can fight our own battles, but it is God who fights our battles for us.

Do not forget the covenant I have made with you, and do not worship other gods. Rather, worship the Lord your God; it is he who will deliver you from the hand of all your enemies.

2 Kings 17:38-39

David would not go into battle until he was sure that God was with him. He understood this principle.

As for God, his way is perfect:
*   The Lord's word is flawless;*
*   he shields all who take refuge in Him.*
For who is God besides the Lord?
*   And who is the Rock except our God?*
It is God who arms me with strength
*   and keeps my way secure.*
He is the God who avenges me,
*   who subdues nations under me.*

Psalm 18:30--32, 47

Isaiah said that God was his defense, his strength, and his salvation.

Surely God is my salvation;
  I will trust and not be afraid.
The Lord, the Lord himself, is my strength and my defense;
  he has become my salvation.

Isaiah 12:2

David often referred to God as his shield. This means that he felt comfortable hiding behind God. He had faith that his Heavenly Father would shield him from all of life's fiery darts and more.

My shield is God Most High,
  who saves the upright in heart.

Psalm 7:10

David often spoke to God before he made any major moves. He trusted God's judgment and knew that if he was going to depend on God to fight his battles for him, he had better make sure he was in God's will.

Surely God is my help;
  the Lord is the one who sustains me.

Psalm 54:4

Isaiah's confidence in the Sovereign One was strong. He told those who were planning to attack Israel,

Devise your strategy, but it will be thwarted;
  propose your plan, but it will not stand,
  for God is with us.

Isaiah 8:10

The prophet Zechariah also trusted God to fight Israel's battles. He boasted,

Then the clans of Judah will say in their hearts, "The people of Jerusalem are strong, because the Lord Almighty is their God."

Zechariah 12:5

God will not only go before you to fight your battles, but he also has your back covered. Isaiah said that God will be your rear guard. There will be no surprises from behind.

But you will not leave in haste
  or go in flight;
for the Lord will go before you,
the God of Israel will be your rear guard.

Isaiah 52:12

Many depend on their crops for food and prosperity. We need God for that too,

So neither the one who plants nor the one who waters is anything, but only God, who makes things grow.

1 Corinthians 3:7

Be glad, people of Zion,
  rejoice in the Lord your God,
for he has given you the autumn rains
  because he is faithful.
He sends you abundant showers,
  both autumn and spring rains, as before.

Joel 2:23

Even when we design a house and build it, it is only because God allows it. He is the builder of everything.

For every house is built by someone, but God is the builder of everything.
Hebrews 3:4

We may secretly resent that God is taking credit for everything we do, until we remember how he frustrated the building plans of those who set out to build the tower of Babel, or how he helped Nehemiah and the returning Jews rebuild the walls of Jerusalem in record time. So, we ought not to leave him out of our plans.

If you have been living life on your own and feeling that you have to do it all yourself, you have been missing out. It is no wonder that you are stressed and frustrated. My God wants to simplify your life for you. He wants to take the load off you and carry it for you.

Cast all your anxiety on Him because He cares for you.
1 Peter 5:7

Jesus also told us,

"Take My yoke upon you and learn from Me, for I am gentle and lowly in heart, and you will find rest for your souls. For My yoke is easy and My burden is light."
Matthew 11:29-30 NKJV

You may think that this sounds too good to be true. Why would this great and perfect God care for a person who has done many things that are too unholy to mention? Well, you are in for a surprise. If you will only seek out the Lord, you will find him to be a forgiving God. You see, "All have sinned and fall short of the glory of God" (Romans 3:23). We all deserve to die for our sins.

Like water spilled on the ground, which cannot be recovered, so we must die. But that is not what God desires; rather, He devises ways so that a banished person does not remain banished from him.
2 Samuel 14:14

My God, the Lord, is going to extreme lengths to reach out to sinners. He even gave his Son to die in our stead. Now this unheard-of sacrifice tells me that he is serious about saving us.

Our God is a God who saves;
from the Sovereign Lord comes escape from death.
Psalm 68:20

This is important! Seeking my God, the Lord, is the most important thing we can ever do. You may have wondered why you have been placed on earth. Well, this is it: This is our time to prepare for eternity. How we live now determines how and where we will spend eternity. It is a shame that many are distracted by life itself and never find the true reason for life. It is so important that there is an all-important test at the end — the Judgment. That is why Jesus said,

And if your eye causes you to stumble, pluck it out. It is better for you to enter the kingdom of God with one eye than to have two eyes and be thrown into hell.
Mark 9:47

Jesus came to teach us about the importance of seeking the kingdom of God. Men will tell us that there are other things that are more important.

They say that it is important to get a good education, save money, and eat well to be healthy; but there is nothing more important than seeking God. This should be our number one goal. Jesus and Moses agreed on this.

> *"Man shall not live on bread alone, but on every word that comes from the mouth of God."*
>
> *Matthew 4:4*

Jesus tried to tell us about this over and over.

> *"Therefore, I say to you, do not worry about your life, what you will eat or what you will drink; nor about your body, what you will put on. Is not life more than food and the body more than clothing?*
>
> *"But seek first the kingdom of God and His righteousness, and all these things shall be added to you."*
>
> *Matthew 6:25, 33 NKJV*

Like a relay race, I have been charged to warn you about this. What you do with this information is up to you. If you continue to ignore this information, you will regret it in the end.

> *The righteous will see and fear;*
>   *they will laugh at you, saying,*
> *"Here now is the man*
>   *who did not make God his stronghold*
> *but trusted in his great wealth*
> *and grew strong by destroying others!"*
>
> *Psalm 52:6-7*

I would like for you to get to know my God, the Lord. He is my guide and my best friend through life. He can see things I cannot see and can make my path straight. For sure...we need him a lot more than we realize.

6
He Is Holy

For I am ADONAI your God; therefore, consecrate yourselves and be holy, for I am holy; and do not defile yourselves.

Leviticus 11:44 CJB

Holiness is an attribute of God we are least familiar with. The Lord himself told us that he is holy. As far as we can understand this word, it means that he is perfect, without sin, undefiled, pure, clean, different. Everything around him must also be set apart and consecrated as holy for his use.

We see how important holiness is to the Lord by the very stringent rules he set up for the priests and the Tabernacle. Everything had to be clean and purified before it could be in his presence.

Moses was told to take off his shoes, because the ground where God was meeting with him was holy. God blessed the Sabbath Day and made it holy because he rested on it. God invites us to be holy, because he is holy.

Holiness is so important to the nature of our God, that he has angels that enforce and ensure this holiness continuously. Just as the lepers were required to cry out, "Unclean! Unclean!" so they would not defile anyone, the angels continuously cry out, "Holy...holy...holy," so no one will think of coming near their God to defile him.

We ought to be glad that our God is holy and without sin. It makes him the only reliable and unchanging being in the world. He sets holiness as the standard or mark to shoot for, and that mark does not change. When he made us in his image, he intended that we would be holy like he is holy, but since sin entered into his creation and defiled it, he remains constant so that we can know how far we have gone away from our intended position. If he changed like we do, he could not help us find our way back.

The Lord is holy and is set apart from sin. Sin to him is like kryptonite to the fictitious Superman. That is why it was such a big deal for Jesus, the sinless Son of God, to take on himself all our sins. He became sin for us. That was a big deal. When the priests killed a sacrifice for the sins of the people, the sacrifice died and did not come alive again. If Jesus did not rise from the grave, it would mean that he had failed in His mission; but because he was holy, he overcame and was able to rise again to live in the presence of the holy God. Now, He is once again holy. He should have lost his powers, but he regained them.

When my God, the Lord, first created this earth, and Adam fell to the deception of the evil one, it did not take long for wickedness to spread. The Lord's holy creation had become defiled. So, God had to destroy the people and the animals and start over with Noah and his family.

> *The Lord saw how great the wickedness of the human race had become on the earth, and that every inclination of the thoughts of the human heart was only evil all the time. The Lord regretted that he had made human beings on the earth, and his heart was deeply troubled. So the Lord said, "I will wipe from the face of the earth the human race I have created—and with them the animals, the birds and the creatures that move along the ground—for I regret that I have made them." But Noah found favor in the eyes of the Lord.*
>
> *Genesis 6:5-8*

That should have worked, but before long they had again chosen to disregard God and worship false gods that they had made for themselves. So, God chose a people for himself. Then he could demonstrate how we ought to live and love. He found a man, Abraham, who had some potential, and took him out of his pagan environment. Then he groomed him for the role of being a witness and an example. He blessed Abraham and his descendants to be "the witnesses."

> *"You are My witnesses," says the Lord,*
> *"And My servant whom I have chosen,*
> *That you may know and believe Me,*
> *And understand that I am He.*
> *Before Me there was no God formed,*
> *Nor shall there be after Me."*

Isaiah 43:10 NKJV
He gave them laws to show them the best way to live, and even appeared to them so that they would know him and serve him.

Then Moses and the Levitical priests said to all Israel, "Be silent, Israel, and listen! You have now become the people of the Lord your God. Obey the Lord your God and follow his commands and decrees that I give you today."

Deuteronomy 27:9-10

However, the pull of their sinful nature proved too strong, and it was a struggle to stay faithful to their God, the Lord; just as it has been for Christians, who try to serve him in our time. It should be easier once we get to know him, but we are often distracted. Our Heavenly Father has been very patient with us, even giving his Son to die for our sins, but he does demand our respect.

I like how Robert L. Deffinbaugh described it. He wrote,

Irreverence is a dangerous malady. Even when our motives are sincere and we are actively involved in the worship of God, we must constantly be mindful of the holiness of God and maintain a reverence for Him manifested by our obedience to His instructions and commands.

God told the priests of Judah,

"And now, you priests, this warning is for you. If you do not listen, and if you do not resolve to honor my name," says the Lord Almighty, "I will send a curse on you, and I will curse your blessings. Yes, I have already cursed them, because you have not resolved to honor me."

Malachi 2:1-2

The priests were disrespecting him by not following his instructions. God did give the Jews a lot of instructions for living, but that was a good thing. It was also necessary.

Moses thought they should be the envy of other nations for having these rules.

Observe them carefully, for this will show your wisdom and understanding to the nations, who will hear about all these decrees

and say, "Surely this great nation is a wise and understanding people."
What other nation is so great as to have their gods near them the way
the Lord our God is near us whenever we pray to him? And what other
nation is so great as to have such righteous decrees and laws as this body
of laws I am setting before you today?"

Deuteronomy 4:6-8

Our God, the Lord, is the Creator, and he knew from the beginning what was best for us. For instance, when he told Adam to eat only of the fruits and vegetables of the Garden, He knew this would be the best food for us. Now, after thousands of years of having it our own way and eating meat and a variety of processed foods, we have come back to the realization that God's way promotes better health. Today, vegan and vegetarian diets are all the craze for better health.

Irreverence is sin and an unholy act, but there are certain things God finds detestable. My God, the Lord, is a holy God, and it is a lack of respect to do these things and still expect to have God's favor. He told Samuel,

"'Those who honor me I will honor, but those who despise me will be
disdained.'"

1 Samuel 2:30

If we want a close relationship with our Maker and Master, we should be aware of these things and steer clear of them.

Idolatry

The number one thing God hates is when we worship other gods or give credit to anything or anyone for what he has done for us. It is like when we tell our children that Santa knows when they are good or bad and will bring them gifts at Christmas. We, who are Christians, giving God's attributes to an imaginary Santa… or Satan? We should not be surprised that God is offended by this. He has told us this throughout the Bible. He is the only God, and he is a jealous God. God told Moses,

"See now that I myself am he!
There is no god besides me.
I put to death and I bring to life,
I have wounded and I will heal,

and no one can deliver out of my hand.
I lift my hand to heaven and solemnly swear:
*   As surely as I live forever."*

Deuteronomy 32:39-40

God is holy and cannot tolerate sin or irreverence. Sin has to be destroyed. Moses warned the people of Israel,

Do not follow other gods, the gods of the peoples around you; for the Lord your God, who is among you, is a jealous God and his anger will burn against you, and he will destroy you from the face of the land.

Deuteronomy 6:14-15

You may argue that this practice of honoring Santa Claus at Christmas is a harmless tradition for the fun of the children. However, if we look into it further, we will find that it is a pagan tradition that we have adopted, just as the Israelites adopted pagan traditions from the neighboring pagan nations. Moses had warned them,

The Lord your God will cut off before you the nations you are about to invade and dispossess. But when you have driven them out and settled in their land, and after they have been destroyed before you, be careful not to be ensnared by inquiring about their gods, saying, "How do these nations serve their gods? We will do the same." You must not worship the Lord your God in their way, because in worshiping their gods, they do all kinds of detestable things the Lord hates. They even burn their sons and daughters in the fire as sacrifices to their gods.

See that you do all I command you; do not add to it or take away from it.

Deuteronomy 12:29-32

This is important. It is a simple but effective measure to help us determine what will please God. We are not to add to or take away from the things that God commanded us to do. However, we have been deceived to add some traditions to the Church, and because it is condoned by the Church, we assume it must be okay with God.

We ought to question all traditions and the reasons we do what we do. We should question why we celebrate Easter, which was originally a pagan holiday, worshipping the fertility goddess Ishtar or Astarte. We should question what the Easter bunny has to do with the death and resurrection of Jesus and not follow tradition blindly. Jesus told us how to celebrate His memory:

> *And he took bread, gave thanks and broke it, and gave it to them, saying, "This is my body given for you; do this in remembrance of me."'*
>
> *Luke 22:19*

In other words, Jesus knew we would find other ways to celebrate His memory, so He was saying that communion is the only acceptable thing we need to do to remember Him. He did not want us to add or take away from what God had ordered. God has not ordered us to celebrate the birth of Jesus by giving gifts or hanging greens, yet the Church is very much involved in these pagan rituals. It may even be regarded as heresy to say that Christmas is not a Christian holiday. Nowhere in the Bible did God order us to celebrate the death and resurrection of Jesus with Easter eggs and chocolate bunnies; yet, the Church has blindly embraced these traditions.

If we research the false gods the Lord was constantly rebuking Israel for worshipping, we will learn that Israel also found it hard to break with tradition. They loved the celebrations and were drawn to the festivities they had grown accustomed to in Egypt or had seen done by neighboring nations. They were baking cakes for the same fertility goddess Ishtar. Could these be the same "hot cross buns" we bake today? God told Jeremiah,

> *Do you not see what they are doing in the towns of Judah and in the streets of Jerusalem? The children gather wood, the fathers light the fire, and the women knead the dough and make cakes to offer to the Queen of Heaven. They pour out drink offerings to other gods to arouse my anger.*
>
> *Jeremiah 7:17-18*

Why do we imagine that God will be any less angry with us for participating in these pagan rituals? Adding the name of Jesus to it does not make it acceptable to the Lord. It is a deception from the devil.

Traditions are hard to break. We want to fit in and choosing not to celebrate Christmas and Easter is very difficult when family and friends are still enjoying it right in front of us. Our children may think we are robbing them of the pleasures we once enjoyed when they see their friends enjoying it. I believe it was this pull to fit in that caused the Israelites to continuously choose traditions over the Lord, who had proven himself faithful to them. They loved the Lord, and they said often, "We will do all that the Lord has commanded us to do;" however, through time, they kept falling off the wagon and choosing tradition. We should not be too hard on them because we are guilty of the same thing. Even with all the increase in knowledge, the devil can still outsmart us.

God hates these traditions and will destroy us for them. It was said of Israel,

> *They abandoned the God who made them*
> *and rejected the Rock their Savior.*
> *They made him jealous with their foreign gods*
> *and angered him with their detestable idols.*
> *Deuteronomy 32:15-16*

God loved David's son, Solomon, and give him great wisdom and wealth. He even appeared to him twice. However, Solomon married many foreign wives who influenced him to serve other gods.

> *But King Solomon loved many foreign women, as well as the daughter of Pharaoh: women of the Moabites, Ammonites, Edomites, Sidonians, and Hittites—from the nations of whom the Lord had said to the children of Israel, "You shall not intermarry with them, nor they with you. Surely they will turn away your hearts after their gods." Solomon clung to these in love. And he had seven hundred wives, princesses, and three hundred concubines; and his wives turned away his heart. For it was so, when Solomon was old, that his wives turned his heart after other gods; and his heart was not loyal to the Lord his God, as was the heart of his father David. For Solomon went after Ashtoreth the goddess of the Sidonians, and after Milcom the abomination of the Ammonites. Solomon did evil in the sight of the Lord, and did not fully follow the Lord, as did his father David. Then Solomon built a high place for Chemosh the abomination of Moab, on the hill that is east of Jerusalem, and for Molech the abomination of the people of Ammon. And he did likewise for all his foreign wives, who burned incense and*

sacrificed to their gods.

1 Kings 11:1-8 NKJV

Solomon started out so good. He sought God with all his heart, and the Lord give him the desires of his heart. Festivities and traditions were his downfall. Who would have imagined that Solomon, blessed with so much wisdom, would have disrespected God like that?

> *The Lord became angry with Solomon because his heart had turned away from the Lord, the God of Israel, who had appeared to him twice.*
>
> *1 Kings 11:9*

God cursed Solomon's blessings just like he had told the priests. He took away the kingdom and give most of it to Solomon's servant, leaving one part with his son for David's sake. Sometimes we wonder why God does not give us wealth like he gave to Solomon, but it is because He loves us and does not want to lose us. He knows what is important and that we would probably not handle wealth and remain faithful, so he gives us just enough to keep us faithful in the kingdom.

> *Command those who are rich in this present world not to be arrogant nor to put their hope in wealth, which is so uncertain, but to put their hope in God, who richly provides us with everything for our enjoyment.*
>
> *1 Timothy 6:17*

Jesus taught His disciples regarding this. He asked,

> *"For what will it profit a man if he gains the whole world, and loses his own soul? Or what will a man give in exchange for his soul?"*
>
> *Mark 8:36-37 NKJV*

Solomon said,

> *Give me neither poverty nor riches,*
>   *but give me only my daily bread.*
> *Otherwise, I may have too much and disown you*
>   *and say, 'Who is the Lord?'*
> *Or I may become poor and steal,*
>   *and so dishonor the name of my God.*
>
> *Proverbs 30:8-9*

We must honor God and give him our respect. He would like to have our love as well, but he demands our respect. Today, we see how children disrespect their parents, and the parents want to be their friends so much that they allow it. This will not happen with God. He is merciful and forgiving, but he will not tolerate our continued disrespect.

God said, 'Honor your father and mother' and 'Anyone who curses their father or mother is to be put to death.'
Matthew 15:4

For some prophets dishonoring God meant death.

"But a prophet who presumes to speak in my name anything I have not commanded, or a prophet who speaks in the name of other gods, is to be put to death."
Deuteronomy 18:20

You are probably thinking, "Then why does God allow so-called atheists to speak against him and wicked people to disrespect him?" Do not imagine that they will get away with it. One day, when God has had enough of our insubordination, he will say, "Enough," and step out of Heaven to destroy the wicked. He told Isaiah about it.

See, the day of the Lord is coming
  —a cruel day, with wrath and fierce anger—
to make the land desolate
  and destroy the sinners within it.
The stars of heaven and their constellations
  will not show their light.
The rising sun will be darkened
  and the moon will not give its light.
I will punish the world for its evil,
  the wicked for their sins.
I will put an end to the arrogance of the haughty
  and will humble the pride of the ruthless.
I will make people scarcer than pure gold,
  more rare than the gold of Ophir.
Isaiah 13:9-12

No, we should not take God's mercy and his favor for weakness.

Do you show contempt for the riches of his kindness, forbearance and patience, not realizing that God's kindness is intended to lead you to repentance?

Romans 2:4

Even after God had decided to destroy the people of Noah's day, it took him another 120 years to do it. He is merciful and would have changed his plan if they had repented. He is merciful and forgiving. Daniel spoke about this.

The Lord our God is merciful and forgiving, even though we have rebelled against Him.

Daniel 9:9

The prophet Jonah was also aware of it. He did not want to prophesy that God would destroy Nineveh, and he did not like it when they repented and God forgave them. He thought that he would look like a false prophet. No one would ever really be sure whether he had told the truth. He was more concerned about his reputation than for the people God cared about.

He prayed to the Lord, "Isn't this what I said, Lord, when I was still at home? That is what I tried to forestall by fleeing to Tarshish. I knew that you are a gracious and compassionate God, slow to anger and abounding in love, a God who relents from sending calamity."

Jonah 4:2

You see, God is not anxious for any to perish. He told Ezekiel,

Say to them, 'As surely as I live, declares the Sovereign Lord, I take no pleasure in the death of the wicked, but rather that they turn from their ways and live. Turn! Turn from your evil ways! Why will you die, people of Israel?'

Ezekiel 33:11

The people of Israel did not hate the Lord. They loved to hear from him. The elders seemed to be always before Ezekiel, waiting to hear from their God; but the Lord told Ezekiel that they were all talk but no action.

"As for you, son of man, your people are talking together about you by

the walls and at the doors of the houses, saying to each other, 'Come and hear the message that has come from the Lord.' My people come to you, as they usually do, and sit before you to hear your words, but they do not put them into practice. Their mouths speak of love, but their hearts are greedy for unjust gain. Indeed, to them you are nothing more than one who sings love songs with a beautiful voice and plays an instrument well, for they hear your words but do not put them into practice.

Ezekiel 33:30-32

It is the same today. We have mega churches where people flock to church to hear the celebrity preachers. However, they do not get to know and respect the Lord. They have no interest in holiness. The Catholic Church created images of Mary, the mother of Jesus, and have instructed the people to bow down to her and pray to her. She has become an idol to many Christians. Do we imagine that, because the Catholic Church condones it, God will condone that too? Do we think God will be pleased with this practice?

The Sabbath

The Lord, our God, also declared the seventh day of the week to be holy. He called it Sabbath and requires us to keep it holy. We are to rest on this Sabbath Day, because he rested on the seventh day after creating the earth.

The seventh day is a sabbath to the Lord your God. On it you shall not do any work, neither you, nor your son or daughter, nor your male or female servant, nor your animals, nor any foreigner residing in your towns. For in six days the Lord made the heavens and the earth, the sea, and all that is in them, but he rested on the seventh day. Therefore, the Lord blessed the Sabbath day and made it holy.

Exodus 20:10-11

It is so important to God that he said that if anyone was found working on the Sabbath, they were to be put to death.

For six days work is to be done, but the seventh day is a day of sabbath rest, holy to the Lord. Whoever does any work on the Sabbath day is to be put to death.

Exodus 31:15

The Sabbath is a forever covenant that God made with the Israelites. He said they were to keep it for all future generations.

Therefore the children of Israel shall keep the Sabbath, to observe the Sabbath throughout their generations as a perpetual covenant.
                                                        Exodus 31:16 NKJV

Even though the covenant was with Israel, the Lord extends it to anyone who chooses to be identified with him. He told Isaiah.

Do not let the son of the foreigner
Who has joined himself to the Lord
Speak, saying,
"The Lord has utterly separated me from His people";
Nor let the eunuch say,
"Here I am, a dry tree."
For thus says the Lord:
"To the eunuchs who keep My Sabbaths,
And choose what pleases Me,
And hold fast My covenant,
Even to them I will give in My house
And within My walls a place and a name
Better than that of sons and daughters;
I will give them an everlasting name
That shall not be cut off.
                                                        Isaiah 56:3-5 NKJV

Divorce

Divorce and re-marriage is another thing that my God, the Lord, finds detestable. We do not only tolerate it but might find it cute and even romantic. Moses told the people of God,

Then her first husband, who divorced her, is not allowed to marry her again after she has been defiled. That would be detestable in the eyes of the Lord. Do not bring sin upon the land the Lord your God is giving you as an inheritance.
                                                        Deuteronomy 24:4

God does not like divorce. He told Malachi about it.

*"The man who hates and divorces his wife," says the Lord, the God
of Israel, "does violence to the one he should protect," says the Lord
Almighty. So be on your guard, and do not be unfaithful.*

Malachi 2:16

God also finds the gay lifestyle offensive. He warned the Jews about
that.

*Do not have sexual relations with a man as one does with a woman;
that is detestable.*

*For all these things were done by the people who lived in the land before
you, and the land became defiled. And if you defile the land, it will
vomit you out as it vomited out the nations that were before you.*

Leviticus 18:22, 27-28

In fact, God destroyed the ancient cities of Sodom and Gomorrah for
this offense.

If you are beginning to feel a little self-righteous, even more than sexual
immorality, God also hates pride and gossip.

*"God opposes the proud
  but shows favor to the humble."*

James 4:6

*In his pride the wicked man does not seek him;
  in all his thoughts there is no room for God.*

Psalm 10:4

In fact, there are a lot of very common sins that God says are deserving
of death:

*Furthermore, just as they did not think it worthwhile to retain the
knowledge of God, so God gave them over to a depraved mind, so that
they do what ought not to be done. They have become filled with every
kind of wickedness, evil, greed and depravity. They are full of envy,
murder, strife, deceit and malice. They are gossips, slanderers, God-
haters, insolent, arrogant and boastful; they invent ways of doing evil;
they disobey their parents; they have no understanding, no fidelity, no
love, no mercy. Although they know God's righteous decree that those
who do such things deserve death, they not only continue to do these*

very things but also approve of those who practice them.

Romans 1:28-32

We have gone so far away from what God intended for us, that these things seem normal. However, God does not change. He is forever holy, and sin will always be sin to him, regardless of how we view it. Sin must be punished. Unless we accept the blood of Jesus to cleanse us from all sin, we will be forever trying to cover them ourselves. He never does condone sin. So, do not ever get the idea that God accepts some sins.

You sit and speak against your brother;
You slander your own mother's son.
These things you have done, and I kept silent;
You thought that I was altogether like you;
But I will rebuke you
And set them in order before your eyes.

Psalm 50:20-21 NKJV

We cannot hate our family and love God. God would not condone that.

Whoever claims to love God yet hates a brother or sister is a liar. For whoever does not love their brother and sister, whom they have seen, cannot love God, whom they have not seen.

1 John 4:20

He wants our obedience more than our sacrifices. Sacrifice seems like an attempt at bribery if it is not accompanied by obedience. The Lord told Saul,

"Does the Lord delight in burnt offerings and sacrifices
    as much as in obeying the Lord?
To obey is better than sacrifice,
    and to heed is better than the fat of rams.
For rebellion is like the sin of divination,
    and arrogance like the evil of idolatry.
Because you have rejected the word of the Lord,
    He has rejected you as king."

1 Samuel 15:22-23

It is quite simple. God has told us how to live, and we get to choose if we want to obey. When we obey, we choose life; and when we disobey, we choose death. He does not bombard us with these choices every day, because the choice is ours. Moses reminded the Israelites about this.

> *This day I call the heavens and the earth as witnesses against you that I have set before you life and death, blessings and curses. Now choose life, so that you and your children may live and that you may love the Lord your God, listen to his voice, and hold fast to him. For the Lord is your life, and He will give you many years in the land He swore to give to your fathers, Abraham, Isaac and Jacob.*
>
> *Deuteronomy 30:19-20*

God's expectations are not unreasonable. If we honor him as the great God he is, then we will not have a problem doing life his way.

> *He has shown you, O mortal, what is good.*
> *And what does the Lord require of you?*
> *To act justly and to love mercy*
> *and to walk humbly with your God.*
>
> *Micah 6:8*

That sums up God's requirements in a nutshell. If we are humble before him and give him the respect he requires of us, everything else will fall into place.

> *Whoever conceals their sins does not prosper,*
> *but the one who confesses and renounces them finds mercy.*
> *Blessed is the one who always trembles before God,*
> *but whoever hardens their heart falls into trouble.*
>
> *Proverbs 28:13-14*

For those who have ever been irreverent to God, they are deserving of death. However, the Lord is a God of second chances, and he has given his holy and sinless Son to die in our place. Now, the blood of Jesus is like an antidote that, when applied, allows us to once again have the potential to be holy and to live forever in his kingdom.

In God's kingdom, holiness will also be the standard. We will need to live holy if we are to be a part of the kingdom. Zechariah told us about it.

In that day "HOLINESS TO THE LORD" shall be engraved on the bells of the horses. The pots in the Lord's house shall be like the bowls before the altar. Yes, every pot in Jerusalem and Judah shall be holiness to the Lord of hosts. Everyone who sacrifices shall come and take them and cook in them. In that day there shall no longer be a Canaanite in the house of the Lord of hosts.

Zechariah 14:20-21 NKJV

David also told us that only the holy ones will be able to worship God on that holy hill of Zion in the kingdom.

Who may ascend the mountain of the Lord?
  Who may stand in his holy place?
The one who has clean hands and a pure heart,
  who does not trust in an idol or swear by a false god.
They will receive blessing from the Lord
  and vindication from God their Savior.
Such is the generation of those who seek him,
  who seek your face, God of Jacob.

Psalm 24:3-6

God's holiness has eternal consequences. Since his kingdom will last forever, we need to consider this carefully, because forever is a very long time to be estranged from our God, the Lord.

Therefore, since we are receiving a kingdom that cannot be shaken, let us be thankful, and so worship God acceptably with reverence and awe, for our "God is a consuming fire."

Hebrews 12:28-29

7
Talking to the Lord

Enter his gates with thanksgiving
and his courts with praise;
give thanks to him and praise his name.

Psalm 100:4

Solomon wrote in Ecclesiastes:

Do not be quick with your mouth,
do not be hasty in your heart
to utter anything before God.
God is in heaven
and you are on earth,
so let your words be few.

Ecclesiastes 5:2

What prompted Solomon to say this? We have heard of preachers that pray for hours each day, so which is the correct way to communicate with the Lord our God: short precise prayers or long, impressive prayers? If we research the context of Solomon's words, we see that he was speaking about making vows or pledges to God and not paying those vows. The passage reads,

Guard your steps when you go to the house of God. Go near to listen rather than to offer the sacrifice of fools, who do not know that they do wrong.

Do not be quick with your mouth,
do not be hasty in your heart
to utter anything before God

God is in heaven
  and you are on earth,
  so let your words be few.
A dream comes when there are many cares,
  and many words mark the speech of a fool.

When you make a vow to God, do not delay to fulfill it. He has no pleasure in fools; fulfill your vow. It is better not to make a vow than to make one and not fulfill it. Do not let your mouth lead you into sin. And do not protest to the temple messenger, "My vow was a mistake." Why should God be angry at what you say and destroy the work of your hands? Much dreaming and many words are meaningless. Therefore, fear God.

Ecclesiastes 5:1-7

This is great wisdom to live by. We should be careful about what vows we make to God and be sure to pay those vows. We have heard that God is forgiving, but we should not make promises to God and break them. It shows a lack of respect for him. The fear of God is the beginning of wisdom. God's ways are so far above our ways, we should at least be respectful and honorable when we come to talk to him. The death of Jesus on the cross does not give us the right to disrespect the Father.

Solomon called much speech "the sacrifice of fools" (Ecclesiastes 5:1). There is no requirement for long prayers. Jesus thought the long prayers of the Pharisees were pretentious. He said,

"Woe to you, scribes and Pharisees, hypocrites! For you devour widows' houses, and for a pretense make long prayers. Therefore, you will receive greater condemnation."

Matthew 23:14 NKJV

We need to examine our reason for making long prayers. If it is to impress others that we know how to pray, then that is already the wrong reason, and we are on the way to losing God's interest.

The disciples were also very concerned about the right way to talk to God, and they asked Jesus to teach them to pray. He told them right away,

"When you pray, you shall not be like the hypocrites. For they love to pray standing in the synagogues and on the corners of the streets,

that they may be seen by men. Assuredly, I say to you, they have their reward. But you, when you pray, go into your room, and when you have shut your door, pray to your Father who is in the secret place; and your Father who sees in secret will reward you openly. And when you pray, do not use vain repetitions as the heathen do. For they think that they will be heard for their many words.

"Therefore, do not be like them. For your Father knows the things you have need of before you ask Him."

Matthew 6:5-8 NKJV

It is always wise to think before we speak and to limit the words we utter. A wise man once said,

In the multitude of words sin is not lacking,
But he who restrains his lips is wise.

Proverbs 10:19 NKJV

He also said,

He who has knowledge spares his words,
And a man of understanding is of a calm spirit.

Proverbs 17:27 NKJV

It seems clear that God is not impressed with long prayers. He also does not require it.

Sometimes our actions can be more effective than our words at getting the Lord's attention. For instance, when Solomon wanted to get the Lord's attention, he sacrificed one thousand animals. After the sacrifice, that night the Lord appeared to him to ask what he wanted.

And Solomon loved the Lord, walking in the statutes of his father David, except that he sacrificed and burned incense at the high places.

Now the king went to Gibeon to sacrifice there, for that was the great high place: Solomon offered a thousand burnt offerings on that altar. At Gibeon the Lord appeared to Solomon in a dream by night; and God said, "Ask! What shall I give you?"

1 Kings 3:3-5 NKJV

Our actions can get the Lord's attention quicker than lengthy prayers. Having said that, though, there are times when we feel we need to pray through certain situations, and we want to stay before God until we get the victory. However, it is our attitude that matters in these situations not our words. Paul said that we should let the Spirit of God lead our prayer in these circumstances.

> *Likewise, the Spirit also helps in our weaknesses. For we do not know what we should pray for as we ought, but the Spirit Himself makes intercession for us with groanings which cannot be uttered.*
> *Romans 8:26 NKJV*

It is best to let the Spirit of God intercede for us either by praying in tongues or by groanings, especially when we encounter spiritual battles. We do not know how to fight these battles, so we just trust God to fight them for us.

We also do not need to instruct God on what needs to be done in our lives. If we trust him to guide the way, we need only come before him giving thanks and singing praise songs. That is why we are told:

> *Enter his gates with thanksgiving,*
>   *and his courts with praise;*
>   *give thanks to him and praise his name.*
> *Psalm100:4*

David wrote many songs or psalms. The psalms are songs that were written to be sung unto or before God. In this way, we can spend hours each day just praising God. As we work and as we drive to and from work, we can stay in a constant state of praising and worshipping God. We are urged to sing praises to our God constantly. God inhabits our praises. He is present with us when we sing his praises.

> *But You are holy,*
> *Enthroned in the praises of Israel.*
> *Psalm 22:3 NKJV*

David perfected the art of praising God. He thought praise was so important, he set priests in the Temple to sing God's praise every day and all day long. Other good kings also patterned their worship after David's system. He wrote,

> *I will bless the Lord at all times:*

His praise shall continually be in my mouth.

Psalm 34:1 NKJV

As the praise teams sang their praises unto the Lord, the presence of the Lord would often fill the Temple.

It came even to pass, as the trumpeters and singers were as one, to make one sound to be heard in praising and thanking the Lord; and when they lifted up their voice with the trumpets and cymbals and instruments of music, and praised the Lord, saying, For he is good; for his mercy endureth for ever: that then the house was filled with a cloud, even the house of the Lord.

2 Chronicles 5:13 KJV

The songwriters of the Bible seemed to be obsessed with praise. They wrote,

Seven times a day do I praise thee because of thy righteous judgments.

Psalm 119:164 KJV

Every day will I bless thee; and I will praise thy name for ever and ever.

Psalm 145:2 KJV

Praise ye the Lord: for it is good to sing praises unto our God; for it is pleasant; and praise is comely.

Psalm 147:1 KJV

I will sing a new song to You, O God;
On a harp of ten strings I will sing praises to You.

Psalm 144:9 NKJV

When the Israelites met for their feast days, for seven days they would sing praises to the Lord their God.

So the children of Israel who were present at Jerusalem kept the Feast of Unleavened Bread seven days with great gladness; and the Levites and the priests praised the Lord day by day, singing to the Lord, accompanied by loud instruments.

2 Chronicles 30:21 NKJV

I also have no doubt that because they traveled to and from Jerusalem in groups for these feasts, they sang praises to the Lord going to and returning from Jerusalem. It must have been a wonderful time of fellowship and praise. The sons of Korah told us,

> *When I remember these things, I pour out my soul in me: for I had gone with the multitude, I went with them to the house of God, with the voice of joy and praise, with a multitude that kept holyday.*
>
> *Psalm 42:4 KJV*

David was the first praise and worship king and one of the greatest advocates for praising God. One day in the kingdom, we will see and hear him sing praises to God again.

In the New Testament, the apostle Paul also shared the same thoughts on praise. He wrote,

> *Be filled with the Spirit;*
>
> *Speaking to yourselves in psalms and hymns and spiritual songs, singing and making melody in your heart to the Lord;*
>
> *Giving thanks always for all things unto God and the Father in the name of our Lord Jesus Christ.*
>
> *Ephesians 5:18-20 KJV*
>
> *Let the word of Christ dwell in you richly in all wisdom; teaching and admonishing one another in psalms and hymns and spiritual songs, singing with grace in your hearts to the Lord.*
>
> *Colossians 3:16 KJV*

We can spend all day in the presence of the Lord, and we do not need to say long prayers. We make our requests known to God, then we go our way all day long singing praises to him and thanking him for what he has done. By doing this, we can be close to him, experience his awesome presence, and our faith will be built up to believe that he will guide us and provide for us. If you have not tried this, you should.

Songs of praise and thanksgiving can grow our faith in the Father. Since our Father already knows best what we need, we do not have to come before him with a long list of requests every day.

> *Be anxious for nothing, but in everything by prayer and supplication, with thanksgiving, let your requests be made known to God.*

Philippians 4:6 NKJV

The word "supplication" means a humble request for a current need. It is like the prayer Jesus taught his disciples to pray. Jesus prayed, "Give us this day our daily bread." He asked only for the present and not for the future, which he left in God's hands and direction.

Let us look at what Jesus thought prayer to the Heavenly Father should look like. He taught his disciples to pray like this:

'In this manner, therefore, pray:
Our Father in heaven,
Hallowed be Your name.
Your kingdom come.
Your will be done
On earth as it is in heaven.
Give us this day our daily bread.
And forgive us our debts,
As we forgive our debtors.
And do not lead us into temptation,
But deliver us from the evil one.
For Yours is the kingdom and the power and the glory
   forever. Amen.

Matthew 6:9-13 NKJV

Let us examine it closer.

"Our Father in heaven" acknowledges who we are praying to. It should not be to Mary or to Jesus but to the Heavenly Father. We can come directly before his throne in prayer. Jesus himself told us to pray to our Father in Heaven.

"Hallowed be Your name" is a period of praise to God, so we enter into prayer with praise for our Heavenly Father.

"Your kingdom come. Your will be done on earth as it is in heaven." This acknowledges that we are seeking first the kingdom of God. It says that we are looking forward to the day when God's kingdom comes to earth, when He will live and reign in Jerusalem forever.

"Give us this day our daily bread." This is a short supplication for our current daily needs. We do not dwell on it, because we have faith that if we seek first the kingdom of God, He will meet all our needs.

"And forgive us our debts, as we forgive our debtors." Every time we pray, we should remember to confess our sins to God and ask for forgiveness, as well as be reminded that we need to forgive others first.

"And do not lead us into temptation but deliver us from the evil one." This is a much-neglected part of our prayer. Jesus said that we can ask God not to lead us into temptation and to deliver us from evil. He thought this should be included in our prayer. Perhaps that is why we find ourselves in so much temptation and spiritual battles. Job wrote,

> *But he knows the way that I take;*
>   *when he has tested me, I will come forth as gold.*
> *My feet have closely followed his steps;*
>   *I have kept to his way without turning aside.*
>
> *Job 23:10-11*

Perhaps, if he had prayed instead, "Lead me not into temptation, but deliver me from the evil one," he may have avoided the hardships of those tests.

Abraham was tested, and the Israelites were tested in the wilderness. Jesus knew the heart of God and told us that if we pray, God would deliver us from evil. In this way, we may be able to avoid some of the evil things that would befall us through testing and spiritual battles. We know God has the power to do this, so that is why Jesus followed the prayer with:

"For Yours is the kingdom and the power and the glory forever."

The Father is king in the kingdom and has the power and the glory to do as he pleases, to test or not to test us. When Jesus came to the cross, he prayed, "My Father, if it is possible, may this cup be taken from me. Yet not as I will, but as you will" (Matthew 26:39).

Therefore, it does not hurt to ask, and perhaps God may allow us to forego some of these tests and battles. He is able to do it.

Now Jesus is not telling us to use these exact words every time we pray, but He is saying we should pattern our prayers after this prayer. These are the things that should be included in our prayers.

We should always come before our God with humility and with faith. Even though we cannot see God, we should not forget that we are speaking to the holy and almighty Master, Creator and King of the Universe. When Moses came face to face with God, he showed humility by hiding his face. The great "I Am" told him to take off his shoes because the ground he was standing on was holy ground.

> *When the Lord saw that he had gone over to look, God called to him from within the bush, "Moses! Moses!"*
>
> *And Moses said, "Here I am."*
>
> *"Do not come any closer," God said. "Take off your sandals, for the place where you are standing is holy ground." Then He said, "I am the God of your father, the God of Abraham, the God of Isaac and the God of Jacob." At this, Moses hid his face, because he was afraid to look at God.*
>
> *Exodus 3:4-6*

Abraham also was very humble when he spoke with the Lord face to face. Even though he was passionate enough to defend the cause of the righteous before the Lord, he still did it with humility.

> *Then Abraham answered and said, "Indeed now, I who am but dust and ashes have taken it upon myself to speak to the Lord."*
>
> *Genesis 18:27*

Abraham had great favor with God, and God even called him a friend, but he did not forget that God was the Creator and we are but dust. Perhaps that is why many of the faithful followers of the Lord God always started their prayers with a reminder that God was superior and lives in heaven. Let us look at some of the effective prayers of the Bible.

When king Sennacherib of Assyria was making his victory lap after destroying all the neighboring nations, he showed up at the gates of Jerusalem to fight with King Hezekiah and the Jews, and they were very afraid. Here is the prayer Hezekiah prayed to his living God. It was very effective.

> *And Hezekiah prayed to the Lord: "Lord, the God of Israel, enthroned between the cherubim, you alone are God over all the kingdoms of the earth. You have made heaven and earth. Give ear, Lord, and hear; open your eyes, Lord, and see; listen to the words Sennacherib has sent to ridicule the living God.*
>
> *"It is true, Lord, that the Assyrian kings have laid waste these nations and their lands. They have thrown their gods into the fire and destroyed*

*them, for they were not gods but only wood and stone, fashioned by
human hands. Now, Lord our God, deliver us from his hand, so that
all the kingdoms of the earth may know that you alone, Lord, are God."*

2 Kings 19:15-19

We know that this prayer, though short, was very effective. God fought
the battle for them, and they did not even have to use any weapons. He
gave them an overwhelming victory over the Assyrians.

Another effective prayer was the one Solomon prayed at the dedication
of the Temple. Even though it was a long public prayer, it was effective,
because it was not vain repetition. He started the prayer with,

*"O Lord, God of Israel, there is no God like you in all of heaven and
earth. You keep your covenant and show unfailing love to all who walk
before you in wholehearted devotion."*

2 Chronicles 6:14 NLT

At the end of his prayer, the presence of the Lord filled the Temple.

Also, when King Jehoshaphat was faced with war and did not know
what to do, he prayed a short and genuine but very effective prayer.

*Jehoshaphat stood before the community of Judah and Jerusalem in
front of the new courtyard at the Temple of the Lord. He prayed, "O
Lord, God of our ancestors, you alone are the God who is in heaven.
You are ruler of all the kingdoms of the earth. You are powerful and
mighty; no one can stand against you! O our God, did you not drive
out those who lived in this land when your people Israel arrived? And
did you not give this land forever to the descendants of your friend
Abraham? Your people settled here and built this Temple to honor your
name. They said, 'Whenever we are faced with any calamity such as
war, plague, or famine, we can come to stand in your presence before
this Temple where your name is honored. We can cry out to you to save
us, and you will hear us and rescue us.'*

*"And now see what the armies of Ammon, Moab, and Mount Seir are
doing. You would not let our ancestors invade those nations when Israel
left Egypt, so they went around them and did not destroy them. Now
see how they reward us! For they have come to throw us out of your
land, which you gave us as an inheritance. O our God, won't you stop*

them? We are powerless against this mighty army that is about to attack us. We do not know what to do, but we are looking to you for help."

2 Chronicles 20:5-12 NLT

Again, God fought the battle for them and gave them the victory. One thing all these prayers have in common is that they all begin with praise. Their praise served to identify the God they were praying to but also did wonders to build their faith.

Faith

Let us not forget the element of faith in our prayers. King Asa was one of the good kings of Judah, so much so that God gave him rest from war for many years. However, when the Ethiopians brought their million-man army against King Asa and the Jews, who had only a 580,000-man army, Asa did not complain or cower before them. He went out to fight them with only a short and very effective, faith-filled prayer.

Then Asa cried out to the Lord his God, "O Lord, no one but you can help the powerless against the mighty! Help us, O Lord our God, for we trust in you alone. It is in your name that we have come against this vast horde. O Lord, you are our God; do not let mere men prevail against you!"

2 Chronicles 14:11 NLT

The result was that God fought the battle for them and gave them a great victory.

So the Lord struck the Ethiopians before Asa and Judah, and the Ethiopians fled. And Asa and the people who were with him pursued them to Gerar. So the Ethiopians were overthrown, and they could not recover, for they were broken before the Lord and His army. And they carried away very much spoil. Then they defeated all the cities around Gerar, for the fear of the Lord came upon them; and they plundered all the cities, for there was exceedingly much spoil in them. They also attacked the livestock enclosures, and carried off sheep and camels in abundance, and returned to Jerusalem.

2 Chronicles 14:12-15 NKJV

Giving Thanks

A very big part of David's continuous praise to God was giving thanks. When their God, the Lord, did his wonderful works for them, David would write a song to commemorate the event or several events. Each time they sang these songs, it increased their faith in their Heavenly Father. It was like counting or recording their blessings. So many of God's wonderful miracles and loving acts could have been lost if they had not recorded them when they happened. We would not have them today for our faith-building.

However, even when we do not write them down, we ought to give thanks.

> *In everything give thanks: for this is the will of God in Christ Jesus for you.*
>
> *1 Thessalonians 5:18 NKJV*

David took it a step further. Even when we do not have new blessings to thank God for, we should just thank him because He is good and his mercy to us endures forever.

> *Oh, give thanks to the Lord, for He is good!*
> *For His mercy endures forever.*
>
> *1 Chronicles 16:34 NKJV*

David reasoned that we could always find something to thank God for.

> *Oh, that men would give thanks to the Lord for His*
>   *goodness,*
> *And for His wonderful works to the children of men!*
>
> *Psalm 107:8 NKJV*

Every time David would even think of the name of God, he would give thanks.

> *Sing praise to the Lord, you saints of His,*
> *And give thanks at the remembrance of His holy name.*
>
> *Psalm 30:4 NKJV*

Job also did something similar by periodically offering sacrifices for his children just in case they sinned. He did not want to leave their eternity to chance.

> *In the land of Uz there lived a man whose name was Job. This man was blameless and upright; he feared God and shunned evil. He had seven sons and three daughters, and he owned seven thousand sheep, three thousand camels, five hundred yoke of oxen and five hundred donkeys, and had a large number of servants. He was the greatest man among all the people of the East.*
>
> *His sons used to hold feasts in their homes on their birthdays, and they would invite their three sisters to eat and drink with them. When a period of feasting had run its course, Job would make arrangements for them to be purified. Early in the morning he would sacrifice a burnt offering for each of them, thinking, "Perhaps my children have sinned and cursed God in their hearts." This was Job's regular custom.*
>
> *Job 1:1-5*

We should even get up in the middle of the night and give thanks.

> *At midnight I will rise to give thanks to You,*
> *Because of Your righteous judgments.*
>
> *Psalm 119:62 NKJV*

Basically, we ought to give thanks now, while we can, lest we begin to take his goodness and mercies for granted.

> *For in death there is no remembrance of You;*
> *In the grave who will give You thanks?*
>
> *Psalm 6:5 NKJV*

Thanking God is the least the righteous can do. The angels praise him and give him thanks continuously, and we have much, much more to thank him for.

> *Surely the righteous shall give thanks to Your name; The upright shall dwell in Your presence.*
>
> *Psalm 140:13 NKJV*

God Hears Our Prayers

Even when the Israelites were in Egypt in slavery and worshiping the

Egyptian gods, the Lord rejected them for a time, but He still heard their groanings and reached out to save them.

> The Israelites groaned in their slavery and cried out, and their cry for help because of their slavery went up to God. God heard their groaning and he remembered his covenant with Abraham, with Isaac and with Jacob. So, God looked on the Israelites and was concerned about them.
>
> Exodus 2:23-25

The hardest part of prayer is waiting. We live in time, but God lives in eternity, and a thousand years is like one day to him. God had told Abraham that they would spend four hundred tough years in a foreign country, but he would bring them out with great possessions.

> Then the Lord said to him, "Know for certain that for four hundred years your descendants will be strangers in a country not their own and that they will be enslaved and mistreated there. But I will punish the nation they serve as slaves, and afterward they will come out with great possessions."
>
> Genesis 15:13-14

We need to remember that even when it seems that God is not hearing our prayer, he does care and is concerned about us, just as he was for the Israelites. We have to continue to trust him that there is a reason why we need to wait. For the Israelites, it was to allow the Canaanites time to repent. He told Abraham that the sin of the people there had not yet reached its fullness.

> "In the fourth generation your descendants will come back here, for the sin of the Amorites has not yet reached its full measure."
>
> Genesis 15:16

Moses also revealed that the reason it took forty years to make an eleven-day journey to the Promised Land was because God was testing them.

> Remember how the Lord your God led you all the way in the wilderness these forty years, to humble and test you in order to know what was in your heart, whether or not you would keep his commands. He humbled you, causing you to hunger and then feeding you with manna, which

neither you nor your ancestors had known, to teach you that man does
not live on bread alone but on every word that comes from the mouth
of the Lord.

Deuteronomy 8:2-3

God is fair, and because we cannot see the whole picture, we get frustrated and do not want to wait. However, there may be other people and other reasons involved. It is like when we pray for our football or baseball team to win a game. We forget that there are others praying the same prayer for the other team as well. Usually, our prayer as a fan is selfish and for our temporary pleasure only. There may be a team member on the other team whose job depends on it, and his family and friends are also praying that his team will win. We need to trust God to make the right decision. Some may say that God does not have a hand in these games, but God is answering prayers all the time, and he does care about every part of our existence. That is why David wrote,

> *Listen to my words, Lord,*
>   *consider my lament.*
> *Hear my cry for help,*
>   *my King and my God,*
>   *for to you I pray.*
> *In the morning, Lord, you hear my voice;*
>   *in the morning I lay my requests before you*
>   *and wait expectantly.*

Psalm 5:1-3

Our understanding of global affairs and eternal affairs is limited, so we need to trust that God knows better. Sometimes it may mean we have to wait or even that we have to accept a no, but if we truly trust God's judgment as Master of the Universe, we can move on and praise him anyway.

> *This is the confidence we have in approaching God: that if we ask*
> *anything according to his will, he hears us. And if we know that he*
> *hears us—whatever we ask—we know that we have what we asked of*
> *him.*

1 John 5:14-15

Another example is when a woman thinks she has met the man of her dreams, and she prays God will give him to her in marriage. However, God knows everything about that man, and he also knows the future. The Lord may already have set aside a prince for her, so what is he to do? If he gives her the person she asks for, she may never reach her full potential, so he will say no because he knows better and has a better person set aside for her. We just need to learn to trust God's judgment, and our lives will have far less drama.

To summarize, our conversations with our God, the Lord, should be thoughtful. We should show fear and respect for him. We should be in a state of faith-building worship all day as we praise and thank him in song or in our hearts for all he has done and will do. Let us not rush in where angels fear to go.

> *Exalt the Lord our God*
> * and worship at his holy mountain,*
> * for the Lord our God is holy.*

Psalm 99:9

The songwriters of old admonish us:

> *Shout for joy to the Lord, all the earth.*
> * Worship the Lord with gladness;*
> * come before him with joyful songs.*
> *Know that the Lord is God.*
> * It is he who made us, and we are his;*
> * we are his people, the sheep of his pasture.*
> *Enter his gates with thanksgiving*
> * and his courts with praise;*
> * give thanks to him and praise his name.*
> *For the Lord is good and his love endures forever;*
> * his faithfulness continues through all generations.*

Psalm 100:1-5

We need to practice this now, so that one day, when we meet him, our praise will come naturally and we will not just stand and stare. We will know him, recognize him, and be filled with the same awe and praise for him. We will not rush up to him and start babbling nonsense like Peter did during Jesus' transfiguration, but with dignity and honor, we will be able to say,

> *"We give thanks to you, Lord God Almighty,*
> *the One who is and who was,*
> *because you have taken your great power*
> *and have begun to reign."*
>
> *Revelation 11:17*

We thank God for King David and the other psalmists for their obsession with praising God. Now, we too can sing praises to God all day long.

> *And my tongue shall speak of thy righteousness and of thy praise all the day long.*
>
> *Psalm 35:28 KJV*

We can boast of our God to others and not be ashamed. It is an honor to know him and to be able to praise him.

> *In God we boast all the day long, and praise thy name for ever. Selah.*
>
> *Psalm 44:8 KJV*

8
His Word Is True

God is not human, that he should lie,
not a human being, that he should change his mind.
Does he speak and then not act?
Does he promise and not fulfill?

Numbers 23:19

Hear, Israel: You are now about to cross the Jordan to go in and
dispossess nations greater and stronger than you, with large cities that
have walls up to the sky. The people are strong and tall—Anakites! You
know about them and have heard it said: "Who can stand up against
the Anakites?" But be assured today that the Lord your God is the one
who goes across ahead of you like a devouring fire. He will destroy
them; he will subdue them before you. And you will drive them out
and annihilate them quickly, as the Lord has promised you.

Deuteronomy 9:1-3

Why should the Israelites believe Moses? He had been promising them that for years. He had taken them from Egypt and brought them out into the wilderness, and many had died in the wilderness and still did not get to the Promised Land. Why should they believe him?

The entire journey across the wilderness should have taken less than two weeks. Now it was forty years later, and even Moses died without seeing the promise fulfilled. I'm sure many were asking, "How much longer, Lord?"

Centuries later, and we see how life repeats itself. Jesus the Son of God was taken up into heaven, and he promised to come back for us; but two thousand years have passed, and we are still waiting. How much longer, Lord? We are trying to hold on, but Christians are being killed for their faith. My mother swore that you were coming back soon, but she has died and gone without seeing your promise fulfilled. So, is your Word dependable?

Yet, when we take a bird's eye view at God's Word, we see that no matter how long it took, God always does what he promises. You see, he is working on a larger scale. He promised Abraham four hundred years in advance that one day he would bring his children back to give them the land that he showed him. Abraham did not even have any children at the time. He even told him exactly how it would happen, and it happened exactly as he said. However, waiting is never a pleasant thing. But we just have to trust him and know that he will always fulfill his Word. God's judgment may be slow in coming, but it is sure to come on those who abuse his children.

It is like waiting to have a baby. We know it will take nine months, but the closer we get to the time to deliver the baby, the more impatient we get.

Jesus promised,

> *"Heaven and earth will pass away, but my words will never pass away."*
> *Mark 13:31*

If he said it, it will come to pass, no matter how long it takes. From God's point of view, it is already done. He lives in eternity, but when we live in time, it is as though it is all happening in slow motion.

> *"For my thoughts are not your thoughts,*
>   *neither are your ways my ways,"*
>   *declares the Lord.*
> *"As the heavens are higher than the earth,*
>   *so are my ways higher than your ways*
>   *and my thoughts than your thoughts.*
> *As the rain and the snow*
>   *come down from heaven,*
> *and do not return to it*
>   *without watering the earth*
>   *and making it bud and flourish,*
> *so that it yields seed for the sower and bread for the eater, so is my word*
>   *that goes out from my mouth:*
>   *it will not return to me empty,*

but will accomplish what I desire
  and achieve the purpose for which I sent it."

Isaiah 55:8-11

If only we can get a glimpse of who God truly is, it would change our whole perspective on life itself. We would see how small and insignificant we really are.

However, just knowing that if we seek him, we can find him, and develop a personal and mutually valuable relationship with him blows my mind.

'Know therefore that the Lord your God is God; he is the faithful God, keeping his covenant of love to a thousand generations of those who love him and keep his commandments.'

Deuteronomy 7:9

Our Father, the Lord, told Noah to build a boat or ark because he was going to destroy the people of his day and all living creatures for their wickedness. Every day, for one hundred and twenty years, Noah faithfully worked at building that ark, even at the expense of looking like a mad man. However, one day, when the time was right, God told him to get into the ark with his family and the animals God sent him, and the promised rain started to fall. Suddenly, it was no longer a laughing matter. The people clamored to get into the ark, but God shut the doors, and it was too late for them.

As for God, his way is perfect:
  The Lord's word is flawless;
  he shields all who take refuge in him.

Psalm 18:30

King Hezekiah was a good and faithful king of Judah, and God prospered the kingdom during his reign, which was between 726 and 697 B.C. When the Babylonians came to visit him, he proudly showed them everything in his kingdom. The prophet Isaiah came to visit him at that time and prophesied that those same Babylonians would return someday and would take all his belongings and the people of Judah away as captives.

Then Isaiah said to Hezekiah, "Hear the word of the Lord Almighty:

The time will surely come when everything in your palace, and all that your predecessors have stored up until this day, will be carried off to Babylon. Nothing will be left, says the Lord. And some of your descendants, your own flesh and blood who will be born to you, will be taken away, and they will become eunuchs in the palace of the king of Babylon."

Isaiah 39:5-7

About seventy-five years after Isaiah disappeared from the prophetic scene, Jeremiah started prophesying that same thing (around 627 B.C.). He stuck with his message for years despite beatings and imprisonment. Then one day, in 586 B.C., it happened just as God had promised. God's promises could span centuries and even the prophet's lifetime. Isaiah did not see this come to pass.

In fact, most of the prophets in the Bible prophesied about things that did not happen in their lifetimes. Many also prophesied about the end time, which has not happened as yet. However, we know that these end-time prophecies will happen, because God's Word is a sure thing. If he said it, it will happen.

Isaiah also prophesied about the birth of Jesus.

Therefore, the Lord Himself will give you a sign: Behold, the virgin shall conceive and bear a Son, and shall call His name Immanuel.

Isaiah 7:14 NKJV

For unto us a Child is born,
Unto us a Son is given;
And the government will be upon His shoulder.
And His name will be called
Wonderful, Counselor, Mighty God,
Everlasting Father, Prince of Peace.

Isaiah 9:6 NKJV

Isaiah lived around seven hundred years before Jesus. So, this prophecy was seven hundred years in the making.

In Daniel 9:24-27, Daniel prophesied that Jesus would come and die for our sins, and after that, the Temple would be destroyed and sacrifices would cease. He prophesied this before the Second Temple was built, and this did not happen until more than six hundred years later. Daniel lived around six hundred years before Jesus was born. In 66 A.D., the Romans burned the Second Temple, and in 135 A.D., they exiled the Jews from Jerusalem and forbade them to practice their religion and offer sacrifices. So, God revealed this to Daniel more than six hundred years in advance.

Let us examine this prophecy in Daniel 9:24-27 closer. We will see how most of these prophecies were not confirmed in the Bible, but history itself confirms that God's Word is true.

> *Seventy weeks have been determined upon thy people, and upon the holy city, for sin to be ended, and to seal up transgressions, and to blot out the iniquities, and to make atonement for iniquities, and to bring in everlasting righteousness, and to seal the vision and the prophet, and to anoint the Most Holy.*
>
> *Daniel 9:24 Septuagint*

This prophecy spoke about the death of Jesus and the shedding of his blood for our sins.

> *And thou shalt know and understand, that from the going forth of the command for the answer and for the building of Jerusalem until Christ the prince there shall be seven weeks, and sixty-two weeks.*
>
> *Daniel 9:25 Septuagint*

This prophecy tells when the seventy weeks of years would start. When a command went forth to find an answer and to rebuild Jerusalem, then the 490-year countdown would start.

> *And then the time shall return, and the street shall be built, and the wall, and the times shall be exhausted.*
>
> *Daniel 9:25 Septuagint*

This is a prophecy that the years would be divided into B.C. and A.D. Since they were not exactly numbering the years backward at that time, Daniel truly had no context for understanding this. He must have thought that this meant that time would end, especially since he was told that time would be exhausted.

> *And after the sixty-two weeks, the anointed one shall be destroyed, and there is no judgment in him.*

Daniel 9:26 Septuagint

The prophecy went on to say that the anointed one, Jesus, would be destroyed even though no fault could truly be found in him.

And he shall destroy the city and the sanctuary with the prince that is coming: they shall be cut off with a flood, and to the end of the war which is rapidly completed he shall appoint the city to desolations.
Daniel 9:26 Septuagint

The prophecy continued to tell that later (66 A.D.), God would destroy the city and the sanctuary using the Prince Titus, the son of Flavius, who would appoint the city of Jerusalem to desolation or destruction.

And one week shall establish the covenant with many: and in the midst of the week my sacrifice and drink-offering shall be taken away.
Daniel 9:27 Septuagint

The war will end quickly with a treaty or covenant, but in the middle of the covenant, it will be broken and additional war will start, the Bar Kokhba revolt (132-135 A.D.), during which time the Jewish religion and religious sacrifices will be banned. In 134 A.D., the Romans exiled the Jews and forbade them to re-enter Jerusalem, offer sacrifices, or practice the Jewish religion.

And on the temple shall be the abomination of desolations; and at the end of time an end shall be put to the desolation.
Daniel 9:27 Septuagint

In the place where the Temple had stood, the Romans erected a building that was an abomination of desolation to the Almighty God. The temple grounds would remain desolate or have abominable buildings there until the end of time, when the abomination will end and the Temple will be rebuilt.

We know now that all of this came to pass just as God told Daniel. Daniel may not have understood it, but now, looking back, we can see how it all happened. Because no person had that knowledge, our God who sees everything from the beginning to the end had to have told this to Daniel.

Ezekiel prophesied so much about the distant future, those who heard him started complaining that he was speaking of things that they did not care about. They wanted to know what would happen in their lifetime.

We often take Bible prophecy for granted and do not realize what an amazing feat it is to be able to tell so accurately about future events that cannot even be imagined by people. God had to do it this way so that we could know that it is from him and his Word is dependable.

Many would argue that the Bible cannot prove itself, but history confirms the Bible. Many of these prophecies came to pass outside of the years of the writing of the Bible. Many are still being fulfilled in our time, and others have yet to be fulfilled in the future.

Samuel, the prophet, priest, and judge said,

> *He who is the Glory of Israel does not lie or change his mind; for he is not a human being, that he should change his mind.*
>
> *1 Samuel 15:29*

The Bible is not just a book of ancient stories. It is a book whereby God reveals mysteries past and present so that we will know and understand his nature and abilities as the Everlasting God. When we see how he has always kept his Word, then we will know for sure that the prophecies of the future are to be taken seriously, and we should run to him and be safe. He is not willing that any should perish, so he reveals his mysteries to us so that we can be saved.

Daniel told King Nebuchadnezzar that God reveals mysteries to us.

> *"But there is a God in heaven who reveals mysteries. He has shown King Nebuchadnezzar what will happen in days to come. Your dream and the visions that passed through your mind as you were lying in bed are these:"*
>
> *Daniel 2:28*

When Daniel revealed the king's dream to him, which he had forgotten, the king agreed with Daniel.

> *The king said to Daniel, "Surely, your God is the God of gods and the Lord of kings and a revealer of mysteries, for you were able to reveal this mystery."*
>
> *Daniel 2:47*

When Daniel showed an interest in what the future could hold, God sent angel after angel to show him what would happen in the future. God

is not trying to hide future things from us. He has inspired the writing of
the Bible, which reveals the message of his coming kingdom. He wants us
to be prepared.

> *He who forms the mountains,*
>   *who creates the wind,*
>   *and who reveals his thoughts to mankind,*
> *who turns dawn to darkness,*
>   *and treads on the heights of the earth—*
> *the Lord God Almighty is his name.*
>
> *Amos 4:13*

My amazing God and Father, the Lord, takes pleasure in revealing
his thoughts to mankind. He wants us to know of major events that will
happen in the end time. These events will affect everyone who has ever
lived and will live. Most of the prophets in the Bible, both major and
minor prophets, prophesied about these events that will happen in the end
time. Even Jesus, the Son of God, said that he was sent to preach about the
kingdom of God that will come to earth in the end time.

> *He said to them, "I must preach the kingdom of God to the other cities
> also, because for this purpose I have been sent."*
>
> *Luke 4:43 NKJV*

Just as the God of Abraham, Isaac, and Jacob had to wait until the sins
of the Canaanites had reached its fullness, even so, on a bigger scale, he is
also waiting for the sins of the people of this world to reach its fullness.
One day, he is going to say, "Enough," step out of heaven, and come close
to destroying the earth. David prophesied about this:

> *In my distress I called upon the Lord,*
> *And cried out to my God;*
> *He heard my voice from His temple,*
> *And my cry came before Him, even to His ears.*
>
> *Then the earth shook and trembled;*
> *The foundations of the hills also quaked and were*
>   *shaken*
> *Because He was angry.*

Smoke went up from His nostrils,
And devouring fire from His mouth;
Coals were kindled by it.
He bowed the heavens also and came down
With darkness under His feet.
And He rode upon a cherub and flew;
He flew upon the wings of the wind.
He made darkness His secret place;
His canopy around Him was dark waters
And thick clouds of the skies.
From the brightness before Him,
His thick clouds passed with hailstones and coals of fire.

The Lord thundered from heaven,
And the Most High uttered His voice,
Hailstones and coals of fire.
He sent out His arrows and scattered the foe,
Lightnings in abundance, and He vanquished them.
Then the channels of the sea were seen,
The foundations of the world were uncovered.
At Your rebuke, O Lord,
*At the blast of the breath of Your nostrils. *

He sent from above, He took me;
He drew me out of many waters.
He delivered me from my strong enemy,
From those who hated me,
For they were too strong for me.
They confronted me in the day of my calamity,
But the Lord was my support.
He also brought me out into a broad place;
He delivered me because He delighted in me.

Psalm 18:6-19 NKJV

Many of David's psalms were written for the end time. In the Septuagint, which is the first translation of the Bible from Hebrew to Greek, they are labeled as "for the end time." In these psalms, he was allowed to experience the chaos of the saints in the tribulation of the end time. Many times, he spoke of God saving him from his enemies. Although David was a warrior and fought in a lot of battles, the details of these songs were not realistic for his time. He said that God was so angry, he caused the foundations of the earth and the bottom of the seas to be exposed. We have never seen God this angry.

David also spoke of God drawing him through waters into a wide place, and this is seen as the rapture we often hear about. David's distress is seen as the tribulation the saints will endure for the last three and a half years before they are raptured. They will cry out to God as they are oppressed and killed, and our God, the Lord, will eventually come and take vengeance on their enemies.

Now we know the reason for the rapture. Just as the Lord protected Noah and his family during the first destruction, as our God pours out his fury on the enemies of his saints, we will be taken into a safe place temporarily for our protection. The righteous dead who will be raised from their graves and the righteous who are still alive will be taken there.

The prophet Zechariah also spoke of this future event in Zechariah 14. It will be a dark and bloody day. However, in verse 12, he tells us why the saints will need to be raptured.

And this shall be the plague with which the Lord will strike all the people who fought against Jerusalem:

Their flesh shall dissolve while they stand on their feet,
Their eyes shall dissolve in their sockets,
And their tongues shall dissolve in their mouths.

Zechariah 14:12 NKJV

Although the prophet Zechariah did not have a name for it, we recognize this now as a nuclear disaster, and in verse 4, Zechariah told us why.

On that day His feet will stand on the Mount of Olives, east of Jerusalem, and the Mount of Olives will be split in two from east to west, forming a great valley, with half of the mountain moving north and half moving south.

Zechariah 14:4

Other prophets identified this event as an earthquake. It will disrupt and detonate nuclear weapons and cause major disaster.

Isaiah said that those remaining should hide in their homes until the Lord's anger had passed.

> *Go, my people, enter your rooms*
>   *and shut the doors behind you;*
> *hide yourselves for a little while*
>   *until his wrath has passed by.*
> *See, the Lord is coming out of his dwelling*
>   *to punish the people of the earth for their sins.*
> *The earth will disclose the blood shed on it;*
>   *the earth will conceal its slain no longer.*
>
> *Isaiah 26:20-21*

One parable that more clearly describes the whole end time event can be found in Revelation 11.

> *"And I will appoint my two witnesses, and they will prophesy for 1,260 days, clothed in sackcloth." They are "the two olive trees" and the two lampstands, and "they stand before the Lord of the earth." If anyone tries to harm them, fire comes from their mouths and devours their enemies. This is how anyone who wants to harm them must die. They have power to shut up the heavens so that it will not rain during the time they are prophesying; and they have power to turn the waters into blood and to strike the earth with every kind of plague as often as they want.*

> *Now when they have finished their testimony, the beast that comes up from the Abyss will attack them and overpower and kill them. Their bodies will lie in the public square of the great city—which is figuratively called Sodom and Egypt—where also their Lord was crucified. For three and a half days some from every people, tribe, language and nation will gaze on their bodies and refuse them burial. The inhabitants of the earth will gloat over them and will celebrate by sending each other gifts because these two prophets had tormented those who live on the earth.*

> *But after the three and a half days the breath of life from God entered them, and they stood on their feet, and terror struck those who saw*

them. Then they heard a loud voice from heaven saying to them, "Come up here." And they went up to heaven in a cloud, while their enemies looked on.

At that very hour there was a severe earthquake and a tenth of the city collapsed. Seven thousand people were killed in the earthquake, and the survivors were terrified and gave glory to the God of heaven.'

Revelation 11:3-13

John told us who the two witnesses represent: "the two olive trees" and the "two lampstands." Earlier, it was revealed that the lampstands represent the church.

"The mystery of the seven stars that you saw in my right hand and of the seven golden lampstands is this: The seven stars are the angels of the seven churches, and the seven lampstands are the seven churches."

Revelation 1:20

Since the lampstands are the churches, then it makes sense that the two olive trees represent the Jews. These are the true witnesses of God's power. God told the Jews,

"You are my witnesses," declares the Lord,
"and my servant whom I have chosen,
so that you may know and believe me."

Isaiah 43:10

In the parable, for the first three and a half years of the tribulation period, the Jews and Christians will fight back by using their God-given powers against anyone who would try to kill them. This will result in them being hated and hunted as witches. In the second half of the tribulation, as the persecution intensifies, they will go into hiding, and the church will be left for dead with no help from the government. Then, at the end of the second three and a half years, they will begin to show signs of life again and will be raptured when God calls them to, "Come up here." This will be followed by a huge earthquake, which will kill a lot of people. Everyone will be struck with fear and will begin to call on the Lord.

Our loving Heavenly Father gave us so much information about these events so far in advance that it must be very important to him. We can be sure that just as every other prophecy in the Bible has come to pass, this one will one day also be fulfilled just as he told us in his Word. He cannot lie. He promised,

"Heaven and earth will pass away, but my words will never pass away."
Mark 13:31

While the Israelites were still captive in Babylon, God spoke to Ezekiel about when he would scatter them among the nations. Then, after many years, he would bring them back to re-populate the Land and form the nation of Israel again. He said it would be for his own sake.

Moreover the word of the Lord came to me, saying: "Son of man, when the house of Israel dwelt in their own land, they defiled it by their own ways and deeds; to Me their way was like the uncleanness of a woman in her customary impurity. Therefore, I poured out My fury on them for the blood they had shed on the land, and for their idols with which they had defiled it. So, I scattered them among the nations, and they were dispersed throughout the countries; I judged them according to their ways and their deeds. When they came to the nations, wherever they went, they profaned My holy name—when they said of them, 'These are the people of the Lord, and yet they have gone out of His land.' But I had concern for My holy name, which the house of Israel had profaned among the nations wherever they went.

"Therefore, say to the house of Israel, 'Thus says the Lord GOD: "I do not do this for your sake, O house of Israel, but for My holy name's sake, which you have profaned among the nations wherever you went. And I will sanctify My great name, which has been profaned among the nations, which you have profaned in their midst; and the nations shall know that I am the Lord," says the Lord GOD, "when I am hallowed in you before their eyes. For I will take you from among the nations, gather you out of all countries, and bring you into your own land."

"Then you will remember your evil ways and your deeds that were not good; and you will loathe yourselves in your own sight, for your iniquities and your abominations."
Ezekiel 36:16-24, 31 NKJV

Some may say that this applies to the exile in Babylon, but the scattering God was most likely speaking about is the exile of 134 A.D., when the Jews were driven out of their land and forbidden to offer sacrifices. For more than eighteen hundred years, they were scattered among many nations. However, in 1948, God brought them back to their land just as he had promised.

The most amazing prophecy for the end time is that one day the Lord will come to earth, live among his creation, and rule this earth from Jerusalem. It will be God's kingdom come to earth.

> *"Sing and rejoice, O daughter of Zion! For behold, I am coming and I will dwell in your midst," says the Lord. "Many nations shall be joined to the Lord in that day, and they shall become My people. And I will dwell in your midst."*
>
> *Zechariah 2:10-11 NKJV*

God also told the prophet Micah about this.

> *"Those who were exiles will become a strong nation. Then I, the Lord, will rule from Jerusalem as their king forever."*
>
> *Micah 4:7 NLT*

The Lord also told Ezekiel about it.

> *The Lord said to me, "Son of man, this is the place of my throne and the place where I will rest my feet. I will live here forever among the people of Israel."*
>
> *Ezekiel 43:7 NLT*

Amazing Lord of all, we thank you that your Word is always true. We can count on it happening just as you said.

9
The Lord Desires a Relationship with You

I know the thoughts that I think toward you, says the Lord, thoughts of
peace and not of evil, to give you a future and a hope.
Jeremiah 29:11 NKJV

My God, the Lord, who is a great and awesome God and who straddles
the past, the present, and the future, has shared his knowledge with us. He
has not hidden it from us. He wants to use his awesome powers to guide
and to bless us. He is a very generous God, who wants to have a loving
relationship with us. Even though he knows all our shortcomings, he still
pursues us. David says that he is constantly looking for those who would
acknowledge and seek him.

The Lord looks down from heaven upon the children of
  men,
To see if there are any who understand, who seek God.
Psalm 14:2

Let us look at what a relationship with God looks like. Moses had a
great relationship with God. He often spoke to the Lord face to face. He
set up a "tent of meeting" to meet with him.

Now Moses used to take a tent and pitch it outside the camp some
distance away, calling it the "tent of meeting." Anyone inquiring of the
Lord would go to the tent of meeting outside the camp. And whenever
Moses went out to the tent, all the people rose and stood at the entrances
to their tents, watching Moses until he entered the tent. As Moses went
into the tent, the pillar of cloud would come down and stay at the
entrance, while the Lord spoke with Moses. Whenever the people saw
the pillar of cloud standing at the entrance to the tent, they all stood

and worshiped, each at the entrance to their tent. The Lord would speak to Moses face to face, as one speaks to a friend. Then Moses would return to the camp, but his young aide Joshua son of Nun did not leave the tent.

Exodus 33:7-11

It is interesting that Moses did not take the easy way out and stay in his tent to speak with God. He did not wait for the Lord to come to him, but it required an effort to meet with the Lord. Even though he was an old man, he would walk a distance to the tent of meeting outside the camp. Making that effort, God would see Moses coming and know that his intention was to meet with him, so he would always meet Moses there. God was looking forward to those meetings as well. Moses even let us eavesdrop on a conversation that he had with the Lord.

Moses said to the Lord, "You have been telling me, 'Lead these people,' but you have not let me know whom you will send with me. You have said, 'I know you by name and you have found favor with me.' If you are pleased with me, teach me your ways so I may know you and continue to find favor with you. Remember that this nation is your people."

The Lord replied, "My Presence will go with you, and I will give you rest."

Then Moses said to him, "If your Presence does not go with us, do not send us up from here. How will anyone know that you are pleased with me and with your people unless you go with us? What else will distinguish me and your people from all the other people on the face of the earth?"

And the Lord said to Moses, "I will do the very thing you have asked, because I am pleased with you and I know you by name."

Exodus 33:12-17

Does the Lord know your name? Do you have a personal relationship with him? When God looks down, are you distinguishable from all the other people on the face of the earth?

It is not a natural thing for us to seek God. Many do not even want to believe there is a God. We cannot see him, so we ignore him. Out of sight…out of mind. David also spoke of this.

In his pride the wicked man does not seek him;
  in all his thoughts there is no room for God.

Psalm 10:4

The fool says in his heart,
  "There is no God."
They are corrupt, their deeds are vile;
  there is no one who does good.

Psalm 14:1

When we do think of it, we can see how God has been extending his arms to us. He built into us an innate knowledge that he exists, so that those who choose to look at the marvelous creation around us and ask some questions like "Who am I?" or "Why do I exist?" can find answers. Paul said,

What may be known about God is plain to them, because God has made it plain to them. For since the creation of the world God's invisible qualities—his eternal power and divine nature—have been clearly seen, being understood from what has been made, so that people are without excuse.

Romans 1:19-20

Then God added his Word in the form of a book that has survived much hostility throughout many generations. In his Word, he has revealed the past and told us where we came from, as well as what to expect in the future, so we can understand how we ought to live our lives. He also included a lot of information about himself.

"I am the Lord," he says,
  "and there is no other.
I publicly proclaim bold promises.
  I do not whisper obscurities in some dark corner.
I would not have told the people of Israel to seek me
  if I could not be found.
I, the Lord, speak only what is true

and declare only what is right."

Isaiah 45:18-19 NLT

Many read the book and say, "Good book," while others read it and say, "Good God." It is the latter group that will set out to seek a relationship with this amazing God. He told Jeremiah,

You will seek Me and find Me, when you search for Me with all your heart.

Jeremiah 29:13 NKJV

Hosea understood this. He said,

It is time to seek the Lord,
Till He comes and rains righteousness on you.

Hosea 10:12 NKJV

Isaiah also understood this. He said,

With my soul I have desired You in the night,
Yes, by my spirit within me I will seek You early;
For when Your judgments are in the earth,
The inhabitants of the world will learn righteousness.

Isaiah 26:9 NKJV

My God, the Lord, wants us to know him. We were not seeking him, so he sought us out.

"I revealed myself to those who did not ask for me;
*   I was found by those who did not seek me.*
To a nation that did not call on my name,
*   I said, 'Here am I, here am I.'"*

Isaiah 65:1

He chose men who would listen to him and told them about himself, so that we could get to know and love him. He came down and spoke with Adam in the cool of the evening. He befriended Abraham and told him what he planned to do. He took Moses up the mountain for forty days and shared much with him. He gave him helpful rules for us to live by, so we could have a better quality of life.

He visited often with the prophets Isaiah, Daniel, and Ezekiel, to tell them about the future and the last days. Every prophet's experience with God the Father was different. He told Jeremiah in Jeremiah 32:27, "I am the Lord, the God of all mankind. Is anything too hard for me?" He told John in a vision, "I am the Alpha and the Omega, ...who is, and who was, and who is to come, the Almighty" (Revelation 1:8).

Our Heavenly Father is seeking a relationship with us, so how do we begin a relationship with the Master, King, and Judge of this universe? What are the benefits of having a relationship with him?

It begins by seeking him. Seeking him means reading his Book, the Bible, that tells about him and his interactions with humans. It means learning about his provision for our salvation through the gift of his Son and repenting of our sins. It means reaching out to him in prayer and learning to trust him more day after day.

The apostle Paul tried to explain this to the philosophers in Athens. He told them,

> *The God who made the world and everything in it is the Lord of heaven and earth and does not live in temples built by human hands. And he is not served by human hands, as if he needed anything. Rather, he himself gives everyone life and breath and everything else. From one man he made all the nations, that they should inhabit the whole earth; and he marked out their appointed times in history and the boundaries of their lands. God did this so that they would seek him and perhaps reach out for him and find him, though He is not far from any one of us. 'For in him we live and move and have our being.'*
>
> *Acts 17: 24-28*

It is not difficult to find the Lord, especially since he is already looking for you.

> *God looks down from heaven*
> * on the entire human race;*
> *he looks to see if anyone is truly wise,*
> * if anyone seeks God.*
>
> *Psalm 53:2 NLT*

He will see the smallest step in his direction, just as when Moses started walking toward the tent of meeting. God knew his thoughts and moved to meet Moses at the door, where he spoke with him face to face. God recognizes the intentional walk in his direction.

When Solomon wanted to get God's attention, he left the city where he lived and traveled to Bethel, where he sacrificed one thousand animals to God. That same night, God came to him and asked what it was that he wanted. We need to make that intentional effort to get God's attention, so there will be no doubt that we are seeking him. It will allow us to stand out from everyone else when God looks down on the human race.

Seeking God means developing a personal relationship with him and watching him change our desires right before our eyes until we love what he loves and we do what he wants us to do. As Hosea said, "Till He comes and rains righteousness on you" (Hosea 10:12 NKJV).

Seeking him means loving and praising him like the psalmists did. They would sing,

> Come, let us sing for joy to the Lord;
>   let us shout aloud to the Rock of our salvation.
> Let us come before him with thanksgiving
>   and extol him with music and song.
> For the Lord is the great God,
>   the great King above all gods.
> In his hand are the depths of the earth,
>   and the mountain peaks belong to him.
> The sea is his, for he made it,
>   and his hands formed the dry land.
> Come, let us bow down in worship,
>   let us kneel before the Lord our Maker;
> for he is our God
>   and we are the people of his pasture,
>   the flock under his care.
> Today, if only you would hear his voice,
>   do not harden your hearts.
>
> *Psalm 95:1-8*

James says that seeking God also involves caring for others. You will find that you have a new-found desire to help others.

Religion that God our Father accepts as pure and faultless is this: to

look after orphans and widows in their distress and to keep oneself from
being polluted by the world.

James 1:27

Paul said it too.

Do not forget to do good and to share with others, for with such sacrifices
God is pleased.

Hebrews 13:16

God told Isaiah,

"Is this not the fast that I have chosen:
To loose the bonds of wickedness,
To undo the heavy burdens,
To let the oppressed go free,

And that you break every yoke?
Is it not to share your bread with the hungry,
And that you bring to your house the poor who are cast out;
When you see the naked, that you cover him,
And not hide yourself from your own flesh?
Then your light shall break forth like the morning,
Your healing shall spring forth speedily,
And your righteousness shall go before you;
The glory of the Lord shall be your rear guard.
Then you shall call, and the Lord will answer;
You shall cry, and He will say, 'Here I am.'

Isaiah 58:6-9 NKJV

It happens naturally that when you seek God, you are changed in the
process. Righteousness is a side effect of seeking God. You learn to love
others because God loves them. Isaiah told us more about this relationship
with the only true God of the Universe.

This is what the Lord says—
  your Redeemer, the Holy One of Israel:
"I am the Lord your God,
  who teaches you what is best for you,
  who directs you in the way you should go."

Isaiah 48:17

Remember, our Heavenly Father sees the past, present, and future all at once, so he knows what is best for us. He can see the pitfalls we should avoid. If he wants to direct me on how to maximize my potential, that is a huge benefit for me. Solomon spoke of this. He said,

Trust in the Lord with all your heart,
And lean not on your own understanding.
In all your ways acknowledge Him,
And He shall direct your paths.

Proverbs 3:5-6 NKJV

Our Lord and Father is a generous God. He has made many wonderful promises for those who would seek him. Paul told us,

And God is able to bless you abundantly, so that in all things at all times, having all that you need, you will abound in every good work.

2 Corinthians 9:8

Without faith it is impossible to please God, because anyone who comes to Him must believe that He exists and that He rewards those who earnestly seek Him.

Hebrews 11:6

The rewards come with the relationship. He promised,

I will give you hidden treasures,
  riches stored in secret places,
so that you may know that I am the Lord,
  the God of Israel, who summons you by name.

Isaiah 45:3

Personally, I refer to these as his "love letters." When we least expect it, here comes one of those blessings, where you know beyond a doubt that it had to be from God. It is like the little love notes mothers write to their children and put in their lunch boxes to remind them they are loved.

Yes, in a personal relationship with our God, the Lord, we will experience what Paul says "He rewards those who *diligently* seek Him" (Hebrews 11:6).NKJV

David also spoke of this.

For the Lord God is a sun and shield;
*   the Lord bestows favor and honor;*
no good thing does he withhold
*   from those whose walk is blameless.*

Psalm 84:11

Solomon also spoke about this.

To the person who pleases him, God gives wisdom, knowledge and
happiness, but to the sinner he gives the task of gathering and storing
up wealth to hand it over to the one who pleases God.

Ecclesiastes 2:26

Paul also said that we cannot even begin to imagine the things God has
prepared for those who love him.

However, as it is written:
"What no eye has seen,
*   what no ear has heard,*
and what no human mind has conceived"—
*   the things God has prepared for those who love him.*

1 Corinthians 2:9

The key words in all these verses are "love him," "please him," and
"diligently seek him." He rewards those who pour themselves into their
relationship with him.

"'You shall love the Lord your God with all your heart, with all your
soul, with all your mind, and with all your strength.' This is the first
commandment."

Mark 12:30 NKJV

We cannot fake it either, because God will know if it is genuine.

"God is spirit, and his worshipers must worship in the Spirit and in
truth."

John 4:24

When we are faithful, he will not forget. He will reward us.

God is not unjust; he will not forget your work and the love you have
shown him as you have helped his people and continue to help them.
Hebrews 6:10

King Hezekiah was a good king in Judah. In fact, he was regarded as
one of the best kings.

Hezekiah trusted in the Lord, the God of Israel. There was no one like
him among all the kings of Judah, either before him or after him.
2 Kings 18:5

When God sent Isaiah to tell Hezekiah to get his house in order because
he was going to die, Hezekiah cried unto God and reminded him that he
had been faithful, so God changed his mind. God told Isaiah,

"Go back and tell Hezekiah, the ruler of my people, 'This is what the
Lord, the God of your father David, says: I have heard your prayer and
seen your tears; I will heal you. On the third day from now you will go
up to the temple of the Lord.'"
2 Kings 20:5

Our loving Father, the Lord, told Malachi that he keeps a record or a
"scroll of remembrance" regarding those who honor him, and they will be
regarded as his treasured possession.

Then those who feared the Lord talked with each other, and the Lord
listened and heard. A scroll of remembrance was written in his presence
concerning those who feared the Lord and honored his name.

"On the day when I act," says the Lord Almighty, "they will be my
treasured possession. I will spare them, just as a father has compassion
and spares his son who serves him. And you will again see the distinction
between the righteous and the wicked, between those who serve God
and those who do not."
Malachi 3:16-18

Jesus, the Son of God, said that those who do God's will are his family.

"Whoever does God's will is my brother and sister and mother."
Mark 3:35

Even when we do not feel worthy, God has not forgotten but will surprise us with a reward like he surprised Cornelius the Centurion.

At Caesarea there was a man named Cornelius, a centurion in what was known as the Italian Regiment. He and all his family were devout and God-fearing; he gave generously to those in need and prayed to God regularly. One day at about three in the afternoon he had a vision. He distinctly saw an angel of God, who came to him and said, "Cornelius!"

Cornelius stared at him in fear. "What is it, Lord?" he asked

The angel answered, "Your prayers and gifts to the poor have come up as a memorial offering before God."

Acts 10:1-4

The Lord had a special delivery for Cornelius. He sent Peter to teach him about God's amazing gift to mankind and to baptize him and his family. Peter told them,

"I now realize how true it is that God does not show favoritism but accepts from every nation the one who fears him and does what is right."

Acts 10:34-35

God sees every step we take in his direction.

Sometimes, when we look over our lives and see our friends and family getting their rewards in promotions and wages, we feel as though we have wasted our lives; but we have to remind ourselves that our reward is yet to come. Isaiah spoke about this.

But I said, "I have labored in vain;
I have spent my strength for nothing at all.
Yet what is due me is in the Lord's hand,
and my reward is with my God."

Isaiah 49:4

Paul said that when God comes, he will expose the motives of our hearts and we will be acknowledged for it.

Therefore judge nothing before the appointed time; wait until the Lord comes. He will bring to light what is hidden in darkness and will expose the motives of the heart. At that time each will receive their praise from God.

1 Corinthians 4:5

We just need to do what is right and know that God will judge it all.

Now all has been heard;
* here is the conclusion of the matter:*
Fear God and keep his commandments,
* for this is the duty of all mankind.*
For God will bring every deed into judgment,
* including every hidden thing,*
* whether it is good or evil.*

Ecclesiastes 12:13-14

In this wonderful relationship, you will find that God will share secrets and mysteries with you. He will give you wisdom and understanding beyond your years.

Solomon said that the fear of the Lord is the beginning of wisdom.

The fear of the Lord is the beginning of wisdom,
* and the knowledge of the Holy One is understanding.*

Proverbs 9:10

He wants to share his knowledge of the future with us. God is not shy. He really wants to be known by us.

Amos' introduction was quite becoming.

He who forms the mountains,
* who creates the wind,*
* and who reveals His thoughts to mankind,*
who turns dawn to darkness,
* and treads on the heights of the earth—*
* the Lord God Almighty is His name.*

Amos 4:13

References

Deffinbaugh, Robert L. 2002. Let Me See They Glory: A Study of the Attributes of God.
https://books.google.com/books?isbn=0737500077

NewCREEations. "How to See Many Amazing Names of God."
https://newcreeations.org/names-of-god/

For questions and further discussion on this topic, check out the following resources:

http://lystramwilliams.wixsite.com/kingdomtalk

http://www.facebook.com/LystraMWilliams/

CPSIA information can be obtained
at www.ICGtesting.com
Printed in the USA
LVHW011159030619
619965LV00003B/1221/P